Design Patterns in .NET

Reusable Approaches in C# and F# for Object-Oriented Software Design

Dmitri Nesteruk

Apress®

Design Patterns in .NET: Reusable Approaches in C# and F# for Object-Oriented Software Design

Dmitri Nesteruk
St. Petersburg, c.St-Peterburg, Russia

ISBN-13 (pbk): 978-1-4842-4365-7   ISBN-13 (electronic): 978-1-4842-4366-4
https://doi.org/10.1007/978-1-4842-4366-4

Managing Director, Apress Media LLC: Welmoed Spahr
Acquisitions Editor: Joan Murray
Development Editor: Laura Berendson
Coordinating Editor: Jill Balzano

Cover designed by eStudioCalamar

Cover image designed by Freepik (www.freepik.com)

Distributed to the book trade worldwide by Springer Science+Business Media New York, 233 Spring Street, 6th Floor, New York, NY 10013. Phone 1-800-SPRINGER, fax (201) 348-4505, e-mail orders-ny@springer-sbm.com, or visit www.springeronline.com. Apress Media, LLC is a California LLC and the sole member (owner) is Springer Science + Business Media Finance Inc (SSBM Finance Inc). SSBM Finance Inc is a **Delaware** corporation.

For information on translations, please e-mail rights@apress.com, or visit http://www.apress.com/rights-permissions.

Apress titles may be purchased in bulk for academic, corporate, or promotional use. eBook versions and licenses are also available for most titles. For more information, reference our Print and eBook Bulk Sales web page at http://www.apress.com/bulk-sales.

Any source code or other supplementary material referenced by the author in this book is available to readers on GitHub via the book's product page, located at www.apress.com/9781484243657. For more detailed information, please visit http://www.apress.com/source-code.

Printed on acid-free paper

Table of Contents

About the Author

Dmitri Nesteruk is a quantitative analyst, developer, course and book author, and an occasional conference speaker. His interests lie in software development and integration practices in the areas of computation, quantitative finance, and algorithmic trading. His technological interests include C# and C++ programming as well as high-performance computing using technologies such as CUDA and field-programmable gate arrays (FPGAs). He has been a C# MVP since 2009.

Introduction

The topic of design patterns sounds dry, academically dull and, in
all honesty, done to death in almost every programming language
imaginable—including programming languages such as JavaScript
that aren't even properly object-oriented programming (OOP)! So why
another book on it? I know that if you're reading this in a bookstore, you
probably have a limited amount of time to decide whether this is worth the
investment.

I decided to write this book to fill a gap left by the lack of patterns
books in the .NET space. Plenty of books have been written over the years,
but not one has attempted to research all the ways in which modern C#
and F# language features can be used to implement design patterns and
present corresponding examples. Having just completed a similar body of
work for C++,[1] I thought it fitting to replicate the process with .NET.

Now, on to design patterns. The original design patterns book[2] was
published with examples in C++ and Smalltalk and, since then, plenty of
programming languages have incorporated certain design patterns directly
into the language. For example, C# directly incorporated the Observer
pattern with its built-in support for events (and the corresponding event
keyword).

Design patterns are also a fun investigation of how a problem can
be solved in many different ways, with varying degrees of technical
sophistication and different sorts of trade-offs. Some patterns are more

---

[1]Dmitri Nesteruk, *Design Patterns in Modern C++* (New York, NY: Apress, 2017).
[2]Erich Gamma, Richard Helm, Raplph Johnson, and John Vlissides, *Design Patterns: Elements of Reusable Object-Oriented Software* (Reading, MA: Addison Wesley, 1994).

or less essential and unavoidable, whereas other patterns are more of a scientific curiosity (but nevertheless are discussed in this book, because I'm a completionist).

Readers should be aware that comprehensive solutions to certain problems often result in overengineering, or the creation of structures and mechanisms that are far more complicated than necessary for most typical scenarios. Although overengineering is a lot of fun (hey, you get to really solve the problem and impress your coworkers), it's often not feasible due to time, cost, and complexity constraints.

Who This Book Is For

This book is designed to be a modern-day update to the classic Gang of Four (GoF, referring to the four authors) book, targeting specifically the C# and F# programming languages. My focus is primarily on C# and the object-oriented paradigm, but I thought it fair to extend the book to cover some aspects of functional programming and the F# programming language.

The goal of this book is to investigate how we can apply the latest versions of C# and F# to the implementation of classic design patterns. At the same time, it's also an attempt to flesh out any new patterns and approaches that could be useful to .NET developers.

Finally, in some places, this book is quite simply a technology demo for C# and F#, showcasing how some of the latest features (e.g., `dynamic`) make difficult problems a lot easier to solve.

On Code Examples

The examples in this book are all suitable for putting into production, but a few simplifications have been made to aid readability:

- I use public fields. This is not a coding recommendation, but rather an attempt to save you time. In the real world, more thought should be given to proper encapsulation and, in most cases, you probably want to use properties instead.

- I often allow too much mutability either by not using `readonly` or by exposing structures in such a way that their modification can cause threading concerns. We cover concurrency issues for a few select patterns, but I haven't focused on each one individually.

- I don't do any sort of parameter validation or exception handling, again to save some space.

You should be aware that most of the examples leverage the latest version of C# and generally use the latest C# language features that are available to developers. For example, I use `dynamic`, pattern matching, and expression-bodied members liberally.

At certain points in time, I reference other programming languages such as C++ or Kotlin. It is sometimes interesting to note how designers of other languages have implemented a particular feature. C# is no stranger to borrowing generally available ideas from other languages, so I mention those when we come to them.

PART I

Introduction

CHAPTER 1

The SOLID Design Principles

SOLID is an acronym that stands for the following design principles (and their abbreviations):

- Single Responsibility Principle (SRP).

- Open-Closed Principle (OCP).

- Liskov Substitution Principle (LSP).

- Interface Segregation Principle (ISP).

- Dependency Inversion Principle (DIP).

These principles were introduced by Robert C. Martin in the early 2000s; in fact, they are just a selection of five principles out of dozens that are expressed in Martin's books and his blog. These five particular topics permeate the discussion of patterns and software design in general, so before we dive into design patterns (I know you're eager), we're going to do a brief recap of what the SOLID principles are all about.

Single Responsibility Principle

Suppose you decide to keep a journal of your most intimate thoughts. The journal has a title and a number of entries. You could model it as follows:

```csharp
public class Journal
{
  private readonly List<string> entries = new List<string>();
  // just a counter for total # of entries
  private static int count = 0;
}
```

Now, you could add functionality for adding an entry to the journal, prefixed by the entry's ordinal number in the journal. You could also have functionality for removing entries (implemented in a very crude way here). This is easy:

```csharp
public void AddEntry(string text)
{
  entries.Add($"{++count}: {text}");
}

public void RemoveEntry(int index)
{
  entries.RemoveAt(index);
}
```

The journal is now usable as:

```csharp
var j = new Journal();
j.AddEntry("I cried today.");
j.AddEntry("I ate a bug.");
```

It makes sense to have this method as part of the Journal class because adding a journal entry is something the journal actually needs to do. It is the journal's responsibility to keep entries, so anything related to that is fair game.

Now, suppose you decide to make the journal persist by saving it to a file. You add this code to the Journal class:

```
public void Save(string filename, bool overwrite = false)
{
  File.WriteAllText(filename, ToString());
}
```

This approach is problematic. The journal's responsibility is to *keep* journal entries, not to write them to disk. If you add the persistence functionality to Journal and similar classes, any change in the approach to persistence (say, you decide to write to the cloud instead of disk) would require lots of tiny changes in each of the affected classes.

I want to pause here and make a point: An architecture that leads to you having to make lots of tiny changes in lots of classes, whether related (as in a hierarchy) or not, is typically a *code smell*—an indication that something's not quite right. Now, it really depends on the situation: If you're renaming a symbol that is being used in a hundred places, I would argue that's generally okay because ReSharper, Rider, or whatever integrated development environment (IDE) you use will actually let you perform a refactoring and have the change propagate everywhere. When you need to completely rework an interface, though, it can be a very painful process!

We therefore state that persistence is a separate *concern*, one that is better expressed in a separate class. We use the term *separation of concerns* (sadly, the abbreviation SoC is already taken) when talking about the general approach of splitting code into separate classes by functionality. In the cases of persistence in our example, we would externalize it like so:

```
public class PersistenceManager
{
  public void SaveToFile(Journal journal, string filename,
                         bool overwrite = false)
  {
    if (overwrite || !File.Exists(filename))
      File.WriteAllText(filename, journal.ToString());
  }
}
```

This is precisely what we mean by *single responsibility*: Each class has only one responsibility, and therefore has only one reason to change. Journal would need to change only if there is something more that needs to be done with respect to in-memory storage of entries; for example, you might want each entry prefixed by a timestamp, so you would change the Add() method to do exactly that. On the other hand, if you wanted to change the persistence mechanic, this would be changed in PersistenceManager.

An extreme example of an anti-pattern[1] that violates the SRP is called a *God Object*. A God Object is a huge class that tries to handle as many concerns as possible, becoming a monolithic monstrosity that is very difficult to work with. Strictly speaking, you can take any system of any size and try to fit it into a single class, but, more often than not, you'd end up with an incomprehensible mess. Luckily for us, God Objects are easy to recognize either visually or automatically (just count the number of methods) and, thanks to continuous integration and source control systems, the responsible developer can be quickly identified and adequately punished.

Open-Closed Principle

Suppose we have an (entirely hypothetical) range of products in a database. Each product has a color and size and is defined as follows:

```
public enum Color
{
  Red, Green, Blue
}
```

---

[1]An *anti-pattern* is a design pattern that also, unfortunately, shows up in code often enough to be recognized globally. The difference between a pattern and an anti-pattern is that anti-patterns are typically patterns of bad design, resulting in code that is difficult to understand, maintain, and refactor.

```
public enum Size
{
  Small, Medium, Large, Yuge
}

public class Product
{
  public string Name;
  public Color Color;
  public Size Size;

  public Product(string name, Color color, Size size)
  {
    // obvious things here
  }
}
```

Now, we want to provide certain filtering capabilities for a given set of products. We make a `ProductFilter` service class. To support filtering products by color, we implement it as follows:

```
public class ProductFilter
{
  public IEnumerable<Product> FilterByColor
    (IEnumerable<Product> products, Color color)
  {
    foreach (var p in products)
      if (p.Color == color)
        yield return p;
  }
}
```

Our current approach of filtering items by color is all well and good, although of course it could be greatly simplified with the use of LINQ. So, our code goes into production but, unfortunately, some time later, the

boss asks us to implement filtering by size, too. So we jump back into
ProductFilter.cs, add the following code, and recompile:

```
public IEnumerable<Product> FilterBySize
  (IEnumerable<Product> products, Size size)
{
  foreach (var p in products)
    if (p.Size == size)
      yield return p;
}
```

This feels like outright duplication, doesn't it? Why don't we just write
a general method that takes a predicate (i.e., a Predicate<T>)? Well, one
reason could be that different forms of filtering can be done in different
ways: For example, some record types might be indexed and need to be
searched in a specific way; some data types are amenable to search on a
Graphics processing units (GPU) whereas others are not.

Furthermore, you might want to restrict the criteria one can filter on.
For example, if you look at Amazon or a similar online store, you are only
allowed to perform filtering on a finite set of criteria. Those criteria can be
added or removed by Amazon if they find that, say, sorting by number of
reviews interferes with the bottom line.

Okay, so our code goes into production but, once again, the boss
comes back and tells us that now there is a need to search by both size and
color. So what are we to do but add another methods?

```
public IEnumerable<Product> FilterBySizeAndColor(
  IEnumerable<Product> products,
  Size size, Color color)
{
  foreach (var p in products)
    if (p.Size == size && p.Color == color)
      yield return p;
}
```

What we want, from this scenario, is to enforce the *open-closed principle* that states that a type is open for extension, but closed for modification. In other words, we want filtering that is extensible (perhaps in a different assembly) without having to modify it (and recompiling something that already works and might have been shipped to clients).

How can we achieve it? Well, first of all, we conceptually separate (SRP!) our filtering process into two parts: a filter (a construct that takes all items and only returns some) and a specification (a predicate to apply to a data element).

We can make a very simple definition of a specification interface:

```
public interface ISpecification<T>
{
  bool IsSatisfied(T item);
}
```

In this code, type T is whatever we choose it to be: It can certainly be a Product, but it can also be something else. This makes the entire approach reusable.

Next up, we need a way of filtering based on ISpecification<T>: This is done by defining, you guessed it, an IFilter<T>:

```
public interface IFilter<T>
{
  IEnumerable<T> Filter(IEnumerable<T> items, ISpecification<T>
  spec);
}
```

Again, all we are doing is specifying the signature for a method called Filter() that takes all the items and a specification, and returns only those items that conform to the specification.

Based on these interface definitions, the implementation of an improved filter is really simple:

```
public class BetterFilter : IFilter<Product>
{
  public IEnumerable<Product> Filter(IEnumerable<Product> items,
                              ISpecification<Product> spec)
  {
    foreach (var i in items)
      if (spec.IsSatisfied(i))
        yield return i;
  }
}
```

Again, you can think of an ISpecification<T> that is being passed in as a strongly typed equivalent of a Predicate<T> that has a finite set of concrete implementations suitable for the problem domain.

Now, here's the easy part. To make a color filter, you make a ColorSpecification:

```
public class ColorSpecification : ISpecification<Product>
{
  private Color color;

  public ColorSpecification(Color color)
  {
    this.color = color;
  }

  public bool IsSatisfied(Product p)
  {
    return p.Color == color;
  }
}
```

Armed with this specification, and given a list of products, we can now filter them as follows:

```
var apple = new Product("Apple", Color.Green, Size.Small);
var tree = new Product("Tree", Color.Green, Size.Large);
var house = new Product("House", Color.Blue, Size.Large);

Product[] products = {apple, tree, house};

var pf = new ProductFilter();
WriteLine("Green products:");
foreach (var p in pf.FilterByColor(products, Color.Green))
  WriteLine($" - {p.Name} is green");
```

This code gets us "Apple" and "Tree" because they are both green. Now, the only thing we have not implemented so far is searching for size *and* color (or, indeed, explaining how you would search for size *or* color, or mix different criteria). The answer is that you simply make a *composite* specification (or a *combinator*). For example, for the logical AND, you can make it as follows:

```
public class AndSpecification<T> : ISpecification<T>
{
  private readonly ISpecification<T> first, second;

  public AndSpecification(ISpecification<T> first,
  ISpecification<T> second)
  {
    this.first = first;
    this.second = second;
  }

  public override bool IsSatisfied(T t)
  {
    return first.IsSatisfied(t) && second.IsSatisfied(t);
  }
}
```

Now, you are free to create composite conditions on the basis of simpler ISpecifications. Reusing the green specification we made earier, finding something green and big is now as simple as this:

```
foreach (var p in bf.Filter(products,
  new AndSpecification<Product>(
    new ColorSpecification(Color.Green),
    new SizeSpecification(Size.Large))))
{
  WriteLine($"{p.Name} is large");
}

// Tree is large and green
```

This was a lot of code to do something seemingly simple, but the benefits are well worth it. The only really annoying part is having to specify the generic argument to AndSpecification—remember, unlike the color and size specifications, the combinator is not constrained to the Product type.

Keep in mind that, thanks to the power of C#, you can simply introduce an operator & (important: note the single ampersand here; && is a by-product) for two ISpecification<T> objects, thereby making the process of filtering by two (or more) criteria somewhat simpler. The only problem is that we need to change from an interface to an abstract class (feel free to remove the leading I from the name).

```
public abstract class ISpecification<T>
{
  public abstract bool IsSatisfied(T p);

  public static ISpecification<T> operator &(
    ISpecification<T> first, ISpecification<T> second)
  {
    return new AndSpecification<T>(first, second);
  }
}
```

If you now avoid making extra variables for size and color specifications, the composite specification can be reduced to a single line:[2]

```
var largeGreenSpec = new ColorSpecification(Color.Green)
                   & new SizeSpecification(Size.Large);
```

Naturally, you can take this approach to extreme by defining extension methods on all pairs of possible specifications:

```
public static class CriteriaExtensions
{
  public static AndSpecification<Product> And(this Color color,
  Size size)
  {
    return new AndSpecification<Product>(
      new ColorSpecification(color),
      new SizeSpecification(size));
  }
}
```

with the subsequent use:

```
var largeGreenSpec = Color.Green.And(Size.Large);
```

However, this would require a set of pairs of all possible criteria, something that is not particularly realistic, unless you use code generation, of course. Sadly, there is no way in C# of establishing an implicit relationship between an enum Xxx and an XxxSpecification.

Figure 1-1 is a diagram of the entire system we've just built.

---

[2]Notice we're using a single & in the evaluation. If you want to use &&, you'll also need to override the true and false operators in ISpecification.

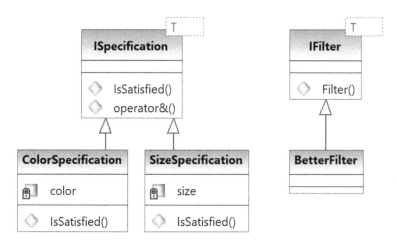

Figure 1-1. *Visual representation of the system built*

So, let's recap what OCP is and how the given example enforces it. Basically, OCP states that you shouldn't need to go back to code you have already written and tested and change it. That is exactly what's happening here! We made ISpecification<T> and IFilter<T> and, from then on, all we have to do is implement either of the interfaces (without modifying the interfaces themselves) to implement new filtering mechanics. This is what is meant by "open for extension, closed for modification."

One thing worth noting is that conformance with OCP is only possible inside an object-oriented paradigm. For example, F#'s discriminated unions are by definition not compliant with OCP because it is impossible to extend them without modifying their original definition.

Liskov Substitution Principle

The Liskov Substitution Principle, named after Barbara Liskov, states that if an interface takes an object of type Parent, it should equally take an object of type Child without anything breaking. Let's take a look at a situation where LSP is broken.

Here's a rectangle; it has width and height and a bunch of getters and setters, and a property getter for calculating the area:

```csharp
public class Rectangle
{
  public int Width { get; set; }
  public int Height { get; set; }

  public Rectangle() {}
  public Rectangle(int width, int height)
  {
    Width = width;
    Height = height;
  }

  public int Area => Width * Height;
}
```

Suppose we make a special kind of Rectangle called a Square. This object overrides the setters to set both width and height:

```csharp
public class Square : Rectangle
{
  public Square(int side)
  {
    Width = Height = side;
  }

  public new int Width
  {
    set { base.Width = base.Height = value; }
  }
```

```
public new int Height
{
  set { base.Width = base.Height = value; }
}
}
```

This approach is *evil*. You cannot see it yet, because it looks very innocent indeed: The setters simply set both dimensions (so that a square always remains a square). What could possibly go wrong? Well, suppose we introduce a method that makes use of a Rectangle:

```
public static void UseIt(Rectangle r)
{
  r.Height = 10;
  WriteLine($"Expected area of {10*r.Width}, got {r.Area}");
}
```

This method looks innocent enough if used with a Rectangle:

```
var rc = new Rectangle(2,3);
UseIt(rc);
// Expected area of 20, got 20
```

However, this innocuous method can seriously backfire if used with a Square instead:

```
var sq = new Square(5);
UseIt(sq);
// Expected area of 50, got 100
```

The preceding code takes the formula Area = Width × Height as an invariant. It gets the width, sets the height to 10, and rightly expects the product to be equal to the calculated area. Calling this method with a Square yields a value of 100 instead of 50. I'm sure you can guess why this is.

The problem here is that although UseIt() is happy to take any Rectangle class, it fails to take a Square because the behaviors inside Square break its operation. How would you fix this issue? Well, one approach would be to simply deprecate the Square class and start treating some Rectangles as special cases. For example, you could introduce an IsSquare property as a way of detecting that a Rectangle is, in fact, a square:

```
public bool IsSquare => Width == Height;
```

As far as setting the properties is concerned, in this case, the solution would be to introduce a uniform SetSize(width,height) method and removing Width/Height setters entirely. This way, you avoid the situation where setting the height via a setter also stealthily changes the width.

Interface Segregation Principle

Here is another contrived example that is nonetheless suitable for illustrating the problem. Suppose you decide to define a multifunction printer, a device that can print, scan, and also fax documents. You define it like so:

```
public class MyFavoritePrinter /* : IMachine */
{
  void Print(Document d) {}
  void Fax(Document d) {}
  void Scan(Document d) {}
};
```

This is fine. Now, suppose you decide to define an interface that needs to be implemented by everyone who also plans to make a multifunction printer. You could use the Extract Interface function in your favorite IDE and you'll get something like the following:

```
public interface IMachine
{
  void Print(Document d);
  void Fax(Document d);
  void Scan(Document d);
}
```

This is a problem because some implementer of this interface might not need scanning or faxing, just printing. Yet you are forcing them to implement those extra features. Sure, they can all be no-op, but why bother with this?

What is particularly annoying about this situation is there is no correct way of leaving things unimplemented. Sure, you can throw an exception, and we even have a dedicated exception precisely for this purpose:

```
public class OldFashionedPrinter : IMachine
{
  public void Print(Document d)
  {
    // this is OK, we can do something here
  }

  public void Fax(Document d)
  {
    throw new System.NotImplementedException();
  }

  public void Scan(Document d)
  {
    // deliberately left blank
  }
}
```

You are still confusing the user, though! They see
OldFashionedPrinter.Fax() as part of the application programming
interface (API), so they can be forgiven for thinking that this type of printer
can fax, too! So what else can you do? Well, you can just leave the extra
methods as no-op (empty), just like the Scan() method earlier. Again, this
approach violates the principle of least surprise (yet another, fairly self-
describing, principle): your users want things to be as predictable as you
can possibly make them. Neither a method that throws, nor a method that
does nothing, is the most predictable solution, even if you make it explicit
in the documentation.

The only option that would categorically work at compile time is the
nuclear option of marking all unnecessary methods obsolete:

```
[Obsolete("Not supported", true)]
public void Scan(Document d)
{
   throw new System.NotImplementedException();
}
```

This will prevent compilation if someone does try to use
OldFashionedPrinter.Scan(). The only issue with this approach is that it
is deeply unidiomatic: the method isn't obsolete, it's unimplemented. Stop
lying to the client!

The ISP suggests you instead split up interfaces, so that implementers
can pick and choose depending on their needs. Because printing and
scanning are different operations (e.g., a scanner cannot print), we define
separate interfaces for these:

```
public interface IPrinter
{
   void Print(Document d);
}
```

```csharp
public interface IScanner
{
  void Scan(Document d);
}
```

Then, a printer can implement *just* the required functionality and nothing else:

```csharp
public class Printer : IPrinter
{
  public void Print(Document d)
  {
    // implementation here
  }
}
```

Similarly, if we want to implement a photocopier, we can do so by implementing the IPrinter and IScanner interfaces:

```csharp
public class Photocopier : IPrinter, IScanner
{
  public void Print(Document d) { ... }
  public void Scan(Document d) { ... }
}
```

Now, if we really want an interface for a multifunction device, we can define it as a combination of the aforementioned interfaces:

```csharp
public interface IMultiFunctionDevice : IPrinter, IScanner //
IFax etc.
{
  // nothing here
}
```

When you come to implement this interface in your concrete multifunction device, this is the interface to use. For example, you could use simple delegation to ensure that Machine reuses the functionality provided by a particular IPrinter and IScanner (this is actually a good illustration of the Decorator pattern):

```
public class MultiFunctionMachine : IMultiFunctionDevice
{
  // compose this out of several modules
  private IPrinter printer;
  private IScanner scanner;

  public MultiFunctionMachine(IPrinter printer, IScanner scanner)
  {
    this.printer = printer;
    this.scanner = scanner;
  }

  public void Print(Document d)
  {
    printer.Print(d);
  }

  public void Scan(Document d)
  {
    scanner.Scan(d);
  }
}
```

So, just to recap, the idea here is to segregate parts of a complicated interface into separate interfaces to avoid forcing clients to implement functionality that they do not really need. Whenever you write a plug-in for some complicated application and you're given an interface with 20 confusing methods to implement with various no-ops and return nulls, more likely than not the API authors have violated the ISP.

Dependency Inversion Principle

The original definition of the Dependency Inversion Principle states the following:[3]

A. High-level modules should not depend on low-level modules. Both should depend on abstractions.

This statement basically means that, if you're interested in logging, your reporting component should not depend on a concrete `ConsoleLogger`, but can depend on an `ILogger` interface. In this case, we are considering the reporting component to be high level (closer to the business domain), whereas logging, being a fundamental concern (kind of like file input/output [I/O] or threading, but not quite) is considered a low-level module.

B. *Abstractions should not depend on details. Details should depend on abstractions.*

This is, once again, restating that dependencies on interfaces or base classes are better than dependencies on concrete types. Hopefully the truth of this statement is obvious, because such an approach supports better configurability and testability, provided you are using a good framework to handle these dependencies for you.

Let's take a look at an example of DIP in action. Suppose we decide to model the genealogical relationship between people using the following definitions:

---

[3]Robert C. Martin, *Agile Software Development, Principles, Patterns, and Practices* (Upper Saddle River, NJ: Prentice Hall, 2002), pp. 127–131.

```
public enum Relationship
{
  Parent,
  Child,
  Sibling
}

public class Person
{
  public string Name;
  // DoB and other useful properties here
}
```

We create a (low-level) class specifically for storing information about relationships. It would look something like the following:

```
public class Relationships // low-level
{
  public List<(Person,Relationship,Person)> relations
    = new List<(Person, Relationship, Person)>();

  public void AddParentAndChild(Person parent, Person child)
  {
    relations.Add((parent, Relationship.Parent, child));
    relations.Add((child, Relationship.Child, parent));
  }
}
```

Now, suppose we want to do some research on the relationships we have captured. For example, to find all the children of John, we create the following (high-level) class:

```
public class Research
{
  public Research(Relationships relationships)
```

23

```
  {
    // high-level: find all of John's children
    var relations = relationships.Relations;
    foreach (var r in relations
      .Where(x => x.Item1.Name == "John"
                  && x.Item2 == Relationship.Parent))
    {
      WriteLine($"John has a child called {r.Item3.Name}");
    }
  }
}
```

The approach illustrated here directly violates DIP because a high-level module Research directly depends on the low-level module Relationships. Why is this bad? Because Research depends directly on the data storage implementation of Relationships: you can see it iterating the list of tuples. What if you wanted to later change the underlying storage of Relationships, perhaps by moving it from a list of tuples to a proper database? Well, you couldn't, because you have high-level modules depending on it.

So what do we want? We want our high-level module to depend on an *abstraction* that, in C# terms, means depending on an interface of some kind. We don't have an interface yet, though. No problem; let's create one:

```
public interface IRelationshipBrowser
{
  IEnumerable<Person> FindAllChildrenOf(string name);
}
```

This interface has a single method for finding all children of a particular person by name. We expect that a low-level module such as Relationships would be able to implement this method and thereby keep its implementation details private:

```
public class Relationships : IRelationshipBrowser // low-level
{
  // no longer public!
  private List<(Person,Relationship,Person)> relations
    = new List<(Person, Relationship, Person)>();

public IEnumerable<Person> FindAllChildrenOf(string name)
{
  return relations
    .Where(x => x.Item1.Name == name
            && x.Item2 == Relationship.Parent)
    .Select(r => r.Item3);
  }
}
```

Now this is something that our Research module can depend on! We can inject an IRelationshipBrowser into its constructor and perform the research safely, without digging into the low-level module's internals:

```
public Research(IRelationshipBrowser browser)
{
  foreach (var p in browser.FindAllChildrenOf("John"))
  {
    WriteLine($"John has a child called {p.Name}");
  }
}
```

Please note that DIP isn't the equivalent of dependency *injection*, which is another important topic in its own right. Dependecy injection can facilitate the application of DIP by simplifying the representation of dependencies, but those two are separate concepts.

CHAPTER 2

The Functional Perspective

The functional paradigm is supported by both the C# and F# languages. Both languages can claim to be multiparadigm because they fully support both object-oriented programming (OOP) and functional programming, although F# has more of a "functional first" mindset with object orientation added for completeness, whereas in C# the integration of functional programming aspects appears to be much more harmonious.

Here we are going to take a very cursory look at functional programming in the C# and F# languages. Some of the material might already be familiar to you; in that case, feel free to skip this part.

Function Basics

First, a note on notation. In this book, I use the words *method* and *function* interchangeably to mean the same thing: a self-contained operation that takes zero or more inputs and has zero or more outputs (return values). I use the word *method* when working exclusively in the C# domain, and likewise use the word *function* when dealing exclusively with the functional domain.

© Dmitri Nesteruk 2019
D. Nesteruk, *Design Patterns in .NET*, https://doi.org/10.1007/978-1-4842-4366-4_2

In C#, functions are not freestanding: They must be members of some class or other. For example, to define integer addition, you must pack the Add() method into some class (let's call it Ops):

```
class Ops
{
  public static int Add(int a, int b)
  {
    return a + b;
  }
}
```

This function is meant to be called as Ops.Add() although you can shorten it to just Add() if you use C#'s import static instruction. Still, this is a particular pain point for mathematicians because, even if you add using static System.Math; to every single file in your project, you still end up having to use uppercase names for functions like Sin(), which is not an ideal situation!

In F#, the situation is drastically different. The preceding addition function can be defined as follows:

```
let add a b = a + b
```

It might appear as if some magic has happened: We didn't define a class, nor did we define any argument types. Yet, if you were to look at the C#-equivalent code, you would see something like the following:

```
[CompilationMapping]
public static class Program
{
  [CompilationArgumentCounts(new int[] {1, 1})]
  public static int add(int a, int b)
  {
```

```
    return a + b;
  }
}
```

As you might have guessed, the static class `Program` got its name from the name of the file the code was in (in this case, `Program.fs`). The types of arguments were chosen as a guesstimate. What if we were to add a call with different argument types?

```
let ac = add "abra" "cadabra"
printfn "%s" ac
```

That code prints "abracadabra," of course, but what is interesting is the code generated. You have guessed it already, haven't you?

```
[CompilationArgumentCounts(new int[] {1, 1})]
public static string add(string a, string b)
{
  return a + b;
}
```

The reason why this is possible is called *type inference*: The compiler figures out which types you are actually using in a function, and tries to accommodate by constructing a function with corresponding parameters. Sadly, this is not a silver bullet. For example, if you were to subsequently add another call, it would fail:

```
let n = add 1 2
// Error: This expression was expected to have type 'string'
but here has type 'int'
```

Functional Literals in C#

It is not always convenient to define functions inside classes: sometimes you want to create a function exactly where you need it; that is, in another function. These sorts of functions are called *anonymous* because they are not given persistent names; instead, the function is stored in a delegate.

The old-fashioned, C# 2.0 way of defining anonymous functions is with the use of a `delegate` keyword, similar to the following:

```
BinaryOperation multiply = delegate(int a, int b)
{ return a * b; };
int x = multiply(2, 3); // 6
```

Of course, since C# 3.0 we have had a much more convenient way of defining the same thing.

```
BinaryOperation multiply = (a, b) => { return a * b; };
```

Notice the disappearance of type information next to a and b: This is type inference at work once again!

Finally, since C# 6 we have had expression-bodied members that allow us to get rid of the `return` keyword in single-statement evaluations, shortening the definition to the following:

```
BinaryOperation multiply = (a, b) => a + b;
```

Of course, anonymous functions are useless if you don't store them somewhere, and as soon as you are storing something, that something needs a *type*. Luckily, we have types of this, too.

Storing Functions in C#

A key feature of functional programming is being able to refer to functions and call them through references. In C#, the simplest way to do this is using delegates.

A *delegate type* is to a function what a class is to an instance. Given our Add() function from earlier, we can define a delegate similar to the following:

```
public delegate int BinaryOperation(int a, int b);
```

A delegate does not have to live inside a C# class: It can exist at a namespace level. So, in a way, you can treat it as a type declaration. Of course, you can also stick a delegate into a class, in which case you can treat it as a *nested* type declaration.

Having a delegate such as this lets us store a reference to a function in a variable:

```
BinaryOperation op = Ops.Add;
int x = op(2, 3);
```

Compared to instances of a class, there is a note that needs to be made here: not only does a delegate instance know *which* function needs to be called, but it also knows the *instance* of the class on which this method should be called. This distinction is critical because it allows us to distinguish, for example, static and nonstatic functions.

Any other function that has the same signature can also be assigned to this delegate, regardless of who its logical owner is. For example, you could define a function called Subtract() virtually anywhere and assign it to the delegate. This includes defining it as an ordinary member function.

```
class Program
{
  static int Subtract(int a, int b) => a - b;
  static void Main(string[] args)
  {
    BinaryOperation op = Subtract;
    int x = op(10, 2); // 8
  }
}
```

However, it can easily be a nested function as well.

```
static void Main(string[] args)
{
  int Multiply(int a, int b) => a * b;
  BinaryOperation op = Multiply;
  int x = op(10, 2); // 20
}
```

It could also be an anonymous delegate or a lambda function:

```
void SomeMethod()
{
  BinaryOperation op = (a, b) => a / b;
  int x = op(10, 2); // 5
}
```

Now, here is the important part: in the majority of cases, defining your own delegates is not necessary. Why? Because the .NET Base Class Library (BCL) comes with predefined delegates of up to 16 parameters in length (C# has no variadic templates[1]) that cover most cases in which you might be interested.

The Action delegate represents a function that does not return a value (is void). Its generic arguments relate to the types of arguments this function takes. So you can write something like:

```
Action doStuff = () => Console.WriteLine("doing stuff!");
doStuff(); // prints "doing stuff!"
```

```
Action<string> printText = x => Console.WriteLine(x);
printText("hello"); // prints "hello"
```

---

[1]Variadic templates are primarily a C++ concept. They allow you to define template (generic) types and methods that take an *arbitrary* number of type arguments, and provide syntax for efficiently iterating the argument type list. .NET generics are implemented differently to C++ templates (their "genericity" is preserved at runtime), so variadics in .NET are not possible.

The generic arguments of Action are needed to specify parameter types. If a function takes no parameters, just use a nongeneric Action.

If your function does need to return a value, then you can use a predefined delegate Func<T1, T2, ..., TR>. This is always generic, where TR has the type of return value. In our case, we could have defined a binary operation as:

```
Func<int, int, int> mul = Multiply;
// or
Func<int, int, int> div = (a, b) => a / b;
```

Together, Action and Func cover all the realistic needs you might encounter for a delegate. Sadly, these delegates themselves cannot be deduced through type inference. In other words, you cannot write

```
var div = (int a, int b) => a / b;
```

expecting div to be of type Func<int, int, int>—this simply will not compile.

Functional Literals in F#

In F#, the process of defining a function is a lot more harmonized. For example, there is no real distinction between the syntax for defining a variable and that of defining a method on the global scope.

```
let add a b = a + b

[<EntryPoint>]
let main argv =
  let z = add
  let result = z 1 2
  0
```

However, the decompiled results of this code are too frightening to show here. That said, it is important to realize that F# does in fact automatically map your function to a type without any extra hints. Instead of mapping it to a Func delegate, though, it maps it to its own type called FSharpFunc.

To understand the reason for FSharpFunc's existence, we need to understand something called *currying*. Currying (nothing to do with Indian food) is an entirely different approach to the way functions are defined and called. Remember when our F# function add a b got turned into a C# equivalent int add(int a, int b)? Well, let me show you a very similar situation where this will *not* happen:

```
let printValues a b =
  printf "a = %i; b = %i" a b
```

What does this compile to? Well, without showing extra levels of gore, the compiler generates, among other things, a class inheriting from FSharpFunc<int, Unit> (Unit can be seen as F#'s equivalent of void) that also happens to have another FSharpFunc<int, Unit> as an invocable member. Why?

Well, to simplify things, your printValues call actually got turned into something like

```
let printValues a =
  let printValues@10-1 b =
    printf "a = %i; b = %i" a b
  return printValues@10-1
```

So, in simplified C# terms, instead of making a function callable as printValues(a,b), we made a function callable as printValues(a)(b).

What is the advantage of this? Well, let's return to our add function:

```
let add a b = a + b
```

We can now use this function to define a new function called `addFive` that adds 5 to a given number. This function can be defined as follows:

```
let addFive x = add 5 x
```

We can now call it as:

```
let z = addFive 5 // z = 10
```

Having this definition forces the compile to express the invocation of any call of `add  x  y` as being equivalent to `add(x)(y)`. However, `add(x)` (without the y) is already prepackaged as a stand-alone `FSharpFunc<int,int>` that itself yields a function that takes a y and adds it to the result. Therefore, the implementation of `addFive` can reuse this function without spawning any further objects!

Now we come back to the question of why F# uses `FSharpFunc` instead of `Func`. The answer is inheritance. Because an invocation of arguments involves not just a single function call but an entire chain, a really useful way of organizing this chain of invocations is by using good old-fashioned inheritance.

Composition

F# has special syntax for calling several functions one after another. In C#, if you need to take the value x and apply to it functions g and then f, you would simply write it as `f(g(x))`. In F#, the possibilities are more interesting.

Let us actually take a look at how these functions could be defined and used. We are going to consider the successive application of two functions, one that adds 5 to a number, the other being one that doubles it.

```
let addFive x = x + 5
let timesTwo x = x * 2

printfn "%i" (addFive (timesTwo 3)) // 11
```

If you think about it, the number 3 in this code goes through a pipeline of operations: First it is fed to `timesTwo`, then to `addFive`. This notion of a pipeline is represented in code through the F# forward pipe and backward pipe operators, which can be used to implement the given operations as follows:

```
printfn "%i" (3 |> timesTwo |> addFive)
printfn "%i" (addFive <| (timesTwo <| 3))
```

Notice that whereas the forward operator `|>` example is very clean, the backward operator `<|` is much less so. The extra brackets are required due to associativity rules.

We might want to define a new function that applies `timesTwo` followed by `addFive` to any argument. Of course, you could simply define it as

```
let timesTwoAddFive x =
  x |> timesTwo |> addFive
```

However, F# also defines function composition operators `>>` (forward) and `<<` (backward) for composing several functions into a single function. Naturally, their arguments must match.

```
let timesTwoAddFive = timesTwo >> addFive
printfn "%i" timesTwoAddFive 3 // 11
```

Functional-Related Language Features

Although not central to the discussion of functional programming, certain features often go with it hand in hand. This includes the following:

- Tail recursion helps with defining algorithms in a recursive fashion.

- Discriminated unions allow very quick definitions of related types with primitive storage mechanics. Sadly, this feature breaks OCP because it is impossible to extend a discriminated union without changing its original definition.

- Pattern matching expands the domain of `if` statements with an ability to match against templates. This is omnipresent in F# (for lists, record types, and others) and is now slowly appearing in C#, too.

- Functional lists are a unique feature (entirely unrelated to `List<T>`), leveraging pattern matching and tail recursion.

These features are synergetic with the functional programming paradigm and can help the implementation of some of the patterns described in this book.

PART II

Creational Patterns

In a managed language such as C#, the process of creating a new object is simple: Just new it up and forget about it. Well, there's stackalloc, but we're talking about objects that need to persist. Now, with the proliferation of dependency injection, another question is whether creating objects manually is still acceptable, or if we should instead defer the creation of all key aspects of our infrastructure to specialized constructs such as factories (more on them in just a moment) or inversion of control containers?

Whichever option you choose, creation of objects can still be a chore, especially if the construction process is complicated or needs to abide by special rules. That's where creational patterns come in: they are common approaches related to the creation of objects.

Just in case you're rusty on the ways an object can be constructed in C#, let's recap the main approaches:

- Invocation of new creates an object on the managed heap. The object doesn't need to be destroyed explicitly because the Garbage Collector (GC) will take care of it for us.

- Stack allocation with stackalloc allocates memory on the stack rather than the heap. Stack-allocated objects only exist in the scope in which they were created and get cleaned up automatically when they go out of scope. This construct can only be used with value types.

- You can allocate unmanaged (native) memory with `Marshal.AllocHGlobal`/`CoTaskMemAlloc` and must explicitly free it with `Marshal.FreeHGlobal`/ `CoTaskMemFree`. This is primarily needed for interoperation with unmanaged code.

Needless to say, some managed component might be working with unmanaged memory behind the scenes. This is one of the main reasons for the existence of the `IDisposable` interface. This interface has a single method, `Dispose()`, that can contain clean-up logic. If you are working with an object that implements `IDisposable`, it might make sense to wrap its use in a `using` statement so that its cleanup code gets executed as soon as the object is no longer needed.

CHAPTER 3

Builder

The Builder pattern is concerned with the creation of *complicated* objects; that is, objects that cannot be built up in a single-line constructor call. These types of objects might themselves be composed of other objects and might involve less-than-obvious logic, necessitating a separate component specifically dedicated to object construction.

I suppose it is worth noting beforehand that, although I said the Builder is concerned with complicated objects, we will be taking a look at a rather trivial example. This is done purely for the purposes of space optimization, so that the complexity of the domain logic doesn't interfere with the reader's ability to appreciate the actual implementation of the pattern.

Scenario

Imagine that we are building a component that renders web pages. A page might consist of just a single paragraph (let's forget all the typical HTML trappings for now), and to generate it, you would probably write something like the following:

```
var hello = "hello";
var sb = new StringBuilder();
sb.Append("<p>");
sb.Append(hello);
sb.Append("</p>");
WriteLine(sb);
```

© Dmitri Nesteruk 2019
D. Nesteruk, *Design Patterns in .NET*, https://doi.org/10.1007/978-1-4842-4366-4_3

This is some serious overengineering, Java-style, but it is a good illustration of one Builder that we already have in the .NET Framework: the StringBuilder. It is, of course, a separate component that is used for concatenating strings. It has utility methods such as AppendLine() so you can append both the text as well as a line break (as in Enrivonment. NewLine). The real benefit to a StringBuilder, though, is that, unlike string concatenation, which results in lots of temporary strings, it just allocates a buffer and fills it up with things that are being appended.

That was too easy, though. Let's try to output a simple unordered list with two items containing the words *hello* and *world*. A very simple implementation might look as follows:

```
var words = new[] { "hello", "world" };
sb.Clear();
sb.Append("<ul>");
foreach (var word in words)
{
  sb.AppendFormat("<li>{0}</li>", word);
}
sb.Append("</ul>");
WriteLine(sb);
```

This does in fact give us what we want, but the approach is not very flexible. How would we change this from a bulleted list to a numbered list? How can we add another item after the list has been created? Clearly, in this rigid scheme of ours, this is not possible once the StringBuilder has been initialized.

We might, therefore, go the OOP route and define an HtmlElement class to store information about each tag:

```
class HtmlElement
{
  public string Name, Text;
```

```
public List<HtmlElement> Elements = new List<HtmlElement>();
private const int indentSize = 2;

public HtmlElement() {}
public HtmlElement(string name, string text)
{
  Name = name;
  Text = text;
}
}
```

That models a single HTML tag that has a name and can also contain either text or a number of children, which are themselves HtmlElements. Armed with this approach, we can now create our list in a more sensible fashion:

```
var words = new[] { "hello", "world" };
var tag = new HtmlElement("ul", null);
foreach (var word in words)
  tag.Elements.Add("li", word);
WriteLine(tag); // calls tag.ToString()
```

This works fine and gives us a more controllable, OOP-driven representation of a list of items. The process of building up each HtmlElement is not very convenient, though, especially if that element has children or some special requirements. Consequently, we turn to the Builder pattern.

Simple Builder

The Builder pattern simply tries to outsource the piecewise construction of an object into a separate class. Our first attempt might yield something like this:

```
class HtmlBuilder
{
  protected readonly string rootName;
  protected HtmlElement root = new HtmlElement();

  public HtmlBuilder(string rootName)
  {
    this.rootName = rootName;
    root.Name = rootName;
  }

  public void AddChild(string childName, string childText)
  {
    var e = new HtmlElement(childName, childText);
    root.Elements.Add(e);
  }

  public override string ToString() => root.ToString();
}
```

This is a dedicated component for building up an HTML element. The constructor of the Builder takes a rootName, which is the name of the root element that is being built: this can be "ul" if we are building an unordered list, "p" if we are making a paragraph, and so on. Internally, we store the root as an HtmlElement, and assign its Name in the constructor, but we also keep hold of the rootName so we can reset the Builder later on if we wanted to.

The AddChild() method is the method that is intended to be used to add additional children to the current element, each child being specified as a name-text pair. It can be used as follows:

```
var builder = new HtmlBuilder("ul");
builder.AddChild("li", "hello");
builder.AddChild("li", "world");
WriteLine(builder.ToString());
```

You'll notice that, at the moment, the AddChild() method is void-returning. There are many things we could use the return value for, but one of the most common uses of the return value is to help us build a fluent interface.

Fluent Builder

Let's change our definition of AddChild() to the following:

```
public HtmlBuilder AddChild(string childName, string childText)
{
  var e = new HtmlElement(childName, childText);
  root.Elements.Add(e);
  return this;
}
```

By returning a reference to the Builder itself, the Builder calls can now be chained. This is called a *fluent interface*:

```
var builder = new HtmlBuilder("ul");
builder.AddChild("li", "hello").AddChild("li", "world");
WriteLine(builder.ToString());
```

The "one simple trick" of returning this allows you to build interfaces where several operations can be crammed into one statement.

Communicating Intent

We have a dedicated Builder implemented for an HTML element, but how will the users of our classes know how to use it? One idea is to simply force them to use the Builder whenever they are constructing an object. Here's what you need to do:

```
class HtmlElement
{
  protected string Name, Text;
  protected List<HtmlElement> Elements = new List<HtmlElement>();
  protected const int indentSize = 2;

  // hide the constructors!
  protected HtmlElement() {}
  protected HtmlElement(string name, string text)
  {
    Name = name;
    Text = text;
  }

  // factory method
  public static HtmlBuilder Create(string name) => new
  HtmlBuilder(name);
}
```

Our approach is two-pronged. First, we have hidden all constructors, so they are no longer available. We have also hidden the implementation details of the Builder itself, something we have not done previously. We have, however, created a Factory Method (this is a design pattern we discuss later) for creating a Builder right out of the HtmlElement, and it's a static method, too! Here's how one would go about using it:

```
var builder = HtmlElement.Create("ul");
builder.AddChild("li", "hello").AddChild("li", "world");
WriteLine(builder);
```

In this example, we are forcing the client to use the static Create() method because there is really no other way to construct an HtmlElement—after all, all the constructors are protected. So the client creates an HtmlBuilder and is then forced to interact with it in the construction of an object. The last line of the listing simply prints the object being constructed.

Let's not forget, though, that our ultimate goal is to build an HtmlElement, and so far we have no way of getting to it! The icing on the cake can be an implementation of implicit operator HtmlElement on the Builder to yield the final value:

```
protected HtmlElement root = new HtmlElement();

public static implicit operator HtmlElement(HtmlBuilder builder)
{
  return builder.root;
}
```

The addition of the operator allows us to write the following:

```
HtmlElement root = HtmlElement
  .Create("ul")
  .AddChildFluent("li", "hello")
  .AddChildFluent("li", "world");
WriteLine(root);
```

Regrettably, there is no way of explicitly telling other users to use the API in this manner. Hopefully the restriction on constructors coupled with the presence of the static Build() function get the user to use the Builder. In addition to the operator, though, it might make sense to also add a corresponding Build() method to HtmlBuilder itself:

```
public HtmlElement Build() => root;
```

Composite Builder

We are going to finish off the discussion of Builder with an example in which multiple builders are used to build up a single object. Let's say we decide to record some information about a person:

```
public class Person
{
  // address
  public string StreetAddress, Postcode, City;

  // employment info
  public string CompanyName, Position;
  public int AnnualIncome;
}
```

There are two aspects to Person: address and employment information. What if we want to have separate builders for each? How can we provide the most convenient API? To do this, we construct a composite builder. This construction is not trivial, so pay attention. Even though we want separate builders for job and address information, we'll spawn no fewer than three distinct classes.

We'll call the first class PersonBuilder:

```
public class PersonBuilder
{
  // the object we're going to build
  protected Person person; // this is a reference!

  public PersonBuilder() => person = new Person();
  protected PersonBuilder(Person person) => this.person = person;
```

```
public PersonAddressBuilder Lives => new
    PersonAddressBuilder(person);
public PersonJobBuilder Works => new PersonJobBuilder(person);

public static implicit operator Person(PersonBuilder pb)
{
    return pb.person;
}
}
```

This is much more complicated than our simple Builder earlier, so let's discuss each member in turn.

- The reference person is a reference to the object that is being built. This field is marked protected, and this is done deliberately for the sub-builders. It is worth noting that this approach only works for reference types—if person was a struct, we would have unnecessary duplication.

- Lives and Works are properties returning builder facets, those subbuilders that initialize the address and employment information separately.

- operator Person is a trick that we have used before.

One very important point to note is the constructors: instead of just initializing the person reference with a new Person() everywhere, we only do so in the public, parameterless constructor. There is another constructor that takes a reference and saves it—this constructor is designed to be used by inheritors and not by the client, that's why it is protected. Things are set up this way so that a Person is instantiated only once per use of the Builder, even if the subbuilders are used.

Now, let's take a look at the implementation of a subbuilder class:

```
public class PersonAddressBuilder : PersonBuilder
{
  public PersonAddressBuilder(Person person) : base(person)
  {
    this.person = person;
  }

  public PersonAddressBuilder At(string streetAddress)
  {
    person.StreetAddress = streetAddress;
    return this;
  }

  public PersonAddressBuilder WithPostcode(string postcode)
  {
    person.Postcode = postcode;
    return this;
  }

  public PersonAddressBuilder In(string city)
  {
    person.City = city;
    return this;
  }
};
```

As you can see, PersonAddressBuilder provides a fluent interface for building up a person's address. Note that it actually inherits from PersonBuilder (meaning it has acquired the Lives and Works member functions). It has a constructor that takes and stores a reference to the object that is being constructed, so when you use these subbuilders, you are always working with just a single instance of Person; you are now accidentally spawning multiple instances. It is *critical* that the base constructor is called—if it is not, the subbuilder will call the parameterless constructor automatically, causing the unnecessary instantiation of additional Person instances.

As you can guess, PersonJobBuilder is implemented in identical fashion, so I omit it here.

Now comes the moment you have been waiting for: an example of these Builders in action.

```
var pb = new PersonBuilder();
Person person = pb
  .Lives
    .At("123 London Road")
    .In("London")
    .WithPostcode("SW12BC")
  .Works
    .At("Fabrikam")
    .AsA("Engineer")
    .Earning(123000);

WriteLine(person);
// StreetAddress: 123 London Road, Postcode: SW12BC, City: London,
// CompanyName: Fabrikam, Position: Engineer, AnnualIncome: 123000
```

Can you see what is happening here? We make a Builder, and then use the Lives property to get us a PersonAddressBuilder, but once we're done initializing the address information, we simply call Works and switch to using a PersonJobBuilder instead. Just in case you need a visual illustration of what we just did, it's rather uncomplicated, as shown in Figure 3-1.

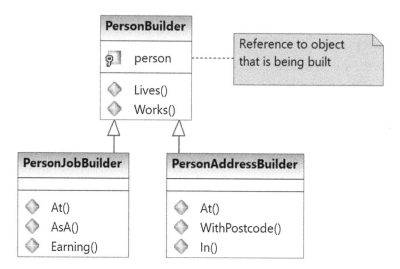

Figure 3-1. *UML representation of the abstract builder and the two sub-builders*

When we are done with the building process, we use the same trick as before to get the object being built-up as a `Person`.

There is one fairly obvious downside to this approach: it is not extensible. Generally speaking, it is a bad idea for a base class to be aware of its own subclasses, yet this is precisely what is happening here: `PersonBuilder` is aware of its own children by exposing them through special APIs. If you wanted to have an additional subbuilder (say, a `PersonEarningsBuilder`), you would have to break OCP and edit `PersonBuilder` directly; you cannot simply subclass it to add an interface member.

Builder Parameter

As I have demonstrated, the only way to coerce the client to use a Builder rather than constructing the object directly is to make the object's constructors inaccessible. There are situations, however, when you want to explicitly force the user to interact with the Builder.

For example, suppose you have an API for sending e-mails, where each e-mail is described internally like this:

```
public class Email
{
  public string From, To, Subject, Body;
  // other members here
}
```

Note that I said *internally* here—you have no desire to let the user interact with this class, perhaps because there is some additional service information stored in it. Keeping it public is fine, though, provided you expose no API that allows the client to send an Email directly. Some parts of the e-mail (e.g., the Subject) are optional, so the object does not have to be fully specified.

You decide to implement a fluent Builder that people will use for constructing an Email behind the scenes. It might appear as follows:

```
public class EmailBuilder
{
  private readonly Email email;
  public EmailBuilder(Email email) => this.email = email;

  public EmailBuilder From(string from)
  {
    email.From = from;
    return this;
  }

  // other fluent members here
}
```

Now to coerce the client to use only the Builder for sending e-mails, you can implement a `MailService` as follows:

```
public class MailService
{
  public class EmailBuilder { ... }

  private void SendEmailInternal(Email email) {}

  public void SendEmail(Action<EmailBuilder> builder)
  {
    var email = new Email();
    builder(new EmailBuilder(email));
    SendEmailInternal(email);
  }
}
```

As you can see, the `SendEmail()` method that clients are meant to use takes a function, not just a set of parameters or a prepackaged object. This function takes an `EmailBuilder` and then is expected to use the Builder to construct the body of the message. Once that is done, we use the internal mechanics of `MailService` to process a fully initialized `Email`.

You'll notice there is a clever bit of subterfuge here: Instead of storing a reference to an e-mail internally, the Builder gets that reference in the constructor argument. We implement it this way so that `EmailBuilder` wouldn't have to expose an `Email` publicly anywhere in its API.

Here's what the use of this API looks like from the client's perspective:

```
var ms = new MailService();
ms.SendEmail(email => email.From("foo@bar.com")
  .To("bar@baz.com")
  .Body("Hello, how are you?"));
```

To make a long story short, the Builder Parameter approach forces the consumers of your API to use a Builder, whether they like it or not.

Fluent Interface Inheritance

One interesting problem that affects not only the fluent Builder but any class with a fluent interface is the problem of inheritance. Is it possible (and realistic) for a fluent Builder to inherit from another fluent Builder? It is, but it's not easy. Here is the problem. Suppose you start out with the following (very trivial) object that you want to build up:

```
public class Person
{
  public string Name;
  public string Position;
}
```

You make a base class Builder that facilitates the construction of Person objects:

```
public abstract class PersonBuilder
{
  protected Person person = new Person();
  public Person Build()
  {
    return person;
  }
}
```

This is followed by a dedicated class for specifying the Person's name:

```
public class PersonInfoBuilder : PersonBuilder
{
  public PersonInfoBuilder Called(string name)
  {
    person.Name = name;
    return this;
  }
}
```

This works, and there is absolutely no issue with it. Now, though, suppose we decide to subclass `PersonInfoBuilder` so as to also specify employment information. You might write something like this:

```
public class PersonJobBuilder : PersonInfoBuilder
{
  public PersonJobBuilder WorksAsA(string position)
  {
    person.Position = position;
    return this;
  }
}
```

Sadly, we have now broken the fluent interface and rendered the entire setup unusable:

```
var me = Person.New
  .Called("Dmitri")
  .WorksAsA("Quant") // will not compile
  .Build();
```

Why won't that code compile? It's simple: `Called()` returns `this`, which is an object of type `PersonInfoBuilder`; that object simply does not have the `WorksAsA()` method!

You might think the situation is hopeless, but it's not: you can design your fluent APIs with inheritance in mind, but it is going to be a bit tricky. Let's take a look at what is involved by redesigning the `PersonInfoBuilder` class. Here is its new incarnation:

```
public class PersonInfoBuilder<SELF> : PersonBuilder
  where SELF : PersonInfoBuilder<SELF>
{
  public SELF Called(string name)
  {
```

```
    person.Name = name;
    return (SELF) this;
  }
}
```

So what happened here? We essentially introduced a new generic argument, SELF. What is more curious is that this SELF is specified to be an inheritor of PersonInfoBuilder<SELF>; in other words, the template argument of the class is required to inherit from this exact class. This might seem like madness, but it is actually a very popular trick for doing CRTP-style (Curiously Recurring Template Pattern is a C++ technique) inheritance in C#. Essentially, we are enforcing an inheritance chain: we are saying that Foo<Bar> is only an acceptable specialization if Foo derives from Bar, and all other cases should fail the where constraint.

The biggest problem in fluent interface inheritance is being able to return a this reference that is typed to the class you are currently in, even if you are calling a fluent interface member of a *base* class. The only way to efficiently propagate this is by having a generic parameter (the SELF) that permeates the entire inheritance hierarchy.

To appreciate this, we need to look at PersonJobBuilder, too:

```
public class PersonJobBuilder<SELF>
  : PersonInfoBuilder<PersonJobBuilder<SELF>>
  where SELF : PersonJobBuilder<SELF>
{
  public SELF WorksAsA(string position)
  {
    person.Position = position;
    return (SELF) this;
  }
}
```

Look at its base class! It's not just an ordinary PersonInfoBuilder as before; instead it's a PersonInfoBuilder<PersonJobBuilder<SELF>>!

So when we inherit from a `PersonInfoBuilder`, we set its `SELF` to `PersonJobBuilder<SELF>` so that all of its fluent interfaces return the correct type, not just the type of the owning class.

Does this make sense? If not, take your time and look through the source code once again. Let's test your understanding. Suppose I introduce another member called `DateOfBirth` and a corresponding `PersonDateOfBirthBuilder`. What class would it inherit from?

If you answered

```
PersonInfoBuilder<PersonJobBuilder<PersonBirthDateBuilder<SELF>>>
```

then you are wrong, but I cannot blame you for trying. Think about it: `PersonJobBuilder` is already a `PersonInfoBuilder`, so that information does not need to be restated explicitly as part of the inheritance type list. Instead, you would define the Builder as follows:

```
public class PersonBirthDateBuilder<SELF>
  : PersonJobBuilder<PersonBirthDateBuilder<SELF>>
  where SELF : PersonBirthDateBuilder<SELF>
{
  public SELF Born(DateTime dateOfBirth)
  {
    person.DateOfBirth = dateOfBirth;
    return (SELF)this;
  }
}
```

The final question we have is this: How do we actually construct such a Builder, considering that it always takes a generic argument? Well, I'm afraid you now need a new *type*, not just a variable. So, for example, the implementation of `Person.New` (the property that starts off the construction process) can be implemented as follows:

```
public class Person
{
```

```
public class Builder : PersonJobBuilder<Builder>
{
  internal Builder() {}
}

public static Builder New => new Builder();

// other members omitted
}
```

This is probably the most annoying implementation detail: the fact that you need to have a non generic inheritor of a recursive generic type to use it.

DSL Construction in F#

Many programming languages (e.g., Groovy, Kotlin, or F#) try to throw in a language feature that will simplify the process of creating domain-specific languages (DSLs), small languages that help describe a particular problem domain. Many applications of such embedded DSLs are used to implement the Builder pattern. For example, if you want to build an HMTL page, you don't have to fiddle with classes and methods directly; instead, you can write something that very much approaches HTML, right in your code!

This is made possible in F# using list comprehensions: the ability to define lists without any explicit calls to Builder methods. For example, if you wanted to support HTML paragraphs and images, you could define the following Builder functions:

```
let p args =
  let allArgs = args |> String.concat "\n"
  [" <p>"; allArgs; "</p>"] |> String.concat "\n"

let img url = "<img src=\"" + url + "\"/>"
```

Notice that whereas the `img` tag only has a single textual parameter, the `<p>` tag accepts a sequence of `args`, allowing it to contain any number of inner HTML elements, including ordinary plain text. We could therefore construct a paragraph containing both text and an image:

```
let html =
  p [
    "Check out this picture";
    img "pokemon.com/pikachu.png"
  ]
printfn "%s" html
```

This outputs

```
<p>
Check out this picture
<img src="pokemon.com/pikachu.png"/>
</p>
```

This approach is used in web frameworks such as WebSharper. There are many variations to this approach, including the use of record types (letting people use curly braces instead of lists), custom operators for specifying plain text, and more.[1]

It is important to note that this approach is only convenient when we are working with an immutable, append-only structure. Once you start dealing with mutable objects (e.g., using a DSL to construct a definition for a Microsoft Project document), you end up falling back into OOP. Sure, the end-result DSL syntax is still very convenient to use, but the plumbing required to make it work is anything but pretty.

---

[1]For an example, see Tomas Petricek's snippet for F# HTML-constructing DSL at `http://fssnip.net/hf`.

Summary

The goal of the Builder pattern is to define a component dedicated entirely to piecewise construction of a complicated object or set of objects. We have observed the following key characteristics of a Builder:

- Builders can have a fluent interface that is usable for complicated construction using a single invocation chain. To support this, Builder functions should return `this`.

- To force the user of the API to use a Builder, we can make the target object's constructors inaccessible and then define a static `Create()` function that returns the Builder. (The naming is up to you; you can call it `Make()`, `New()`, or something else.)

- A Builder can be coerced to the object itself by defining the appropriate implicit conversion operator.

- You can force the client to use a Builder by specifying it as part of a parameter function.

- A single Builder interface can expose multiple subbuilders. Through clever use of inheritance and fluent interfaces, one can jump from one Builder to another with ease.

- Inheritance of fluent interfaces (not just for Builders) is possible through recursive generics.

Just to reiterate something that was already mentioned, the use of the Builder pattern makes sense when the construction of the object is a *nontrivial* process. Simple objects that are unambiguously constructed from a limited number of sensibly named constructor parameters should probably use a constructor (or dependency injection) without necessitating use of a Builder as such.

61

CHAPTER 4

Factories

> I had a problem and tried to use Java, now I have a
> ProblemFactory.
>
> —Old Java joke

This chapter covers two GoF patterns: Factory Method and Abstract
Factory. These patterns are closely related, so we discuss them together.
The truth, though, is that the real design pattern is called *Factory* and that
both Factory Method and Abstract Factory are simply variations that are
important, but certainly not as important as the main thing.

Scenario

Let's begin with a motivating example. Suppose you want to store
information about a `Point` in Cartesian (X-Y) space. So you go ahead and
implement something like this:

```
public class Point
{
  private double x, y;

  public Point(double x, double y)
  {
    this.x = x;
```

```
    this.y = y;
  }
}
```

So far, so good. Now, though, you also want to initialize the point from *polar* coordinates instead. You need another constructor with the signature:

```
Point(float r, float theta)
{
  x = r * Math.Cos(theta);
  y = r * Math.Sin(theta);
}
```

Unfortunately, you already have a constructor with two floats, so you cannot have another one.[1] What do you do? One approach is to introduce an enumeration:

```
public enum CoordinateSystem
{
  Cartesian,
  Polar
}
```

Then add another parameter to the point constructor:

```
public Point(double a,
  double b, // names do not communicate intent
  CoordinateSystem cs = CoordinateSystem.Cartesian)
{
```

---

[1]Some programming languages, most notably Objective-C and Swift, do allow overloading of functions that only differ by parameter names. Unfortunately, this idea results in a viral propagation of parameter names in all calls. I still prefer positional parameters most of the time.

```
switch (cs)
{
  case CoordinateSystem.Polar:
    x = a * Math.Cos(b);
    y = a * Math.Sin(b);
    break;
  default:
    x = a;
    y = b;
    break;
}
}
```

Notice how the names of the first two arguments were changed to a and b: we can no longer afford telling the user which coordinate system those values should come from. This is a clear loss of expressivity when compared with using x, y, rho, and theta to communicate intent.

Overall, our constructor design is usable, but ugly. In particular, to add some third co ordinate system, for example, you would need to do the following:

- Give CoordinateSystem a new enumeration value.

- Change the constructor to support the new coordinate system.

There must be a better way of doing this.

Factory Method

The trouble with the constructor is that its name always matches the type. This means we cannot communicate any extra information in it, unlike in an ordinary method. Also, given that the name is always the same, we cannot have two overloads, one taking x,y and another taking r,theta.

So what can we do? Well, how about making the constructor protected[2] and then exposing some static methods for creating new points?

```
public class Point
{
  protected Point(double x, double y)
  {
    this.x = x;
    this.y = y;
  }

  public static Point NewCartesianPoint(double x, double y)
  {
    return new Point(x, y);
  }

  public static Point NewPolarPoint(double rho, double theta)
  {
    return new Point(rho*Math.Cos(theta), rho*Math.Sin(theta));
  }

  // other members omitted
}
```

Each of these static methods is called a Factory Method. All it does is create a Point and return it, the advantages being that both the name of the method and the names of the arguments clearly communicate what kind of coordinates are required.

Now, to create a point, you simply write

```
var point = Point.NewPolarPoint(5, Math.PI / 4);
```

---

[2]Whenever you want to prevent a client from accessing something, I always recommend you make it protected rather than private because then you make the class inheritance-friendly.

From this code, we can clearly surmise that we are creating a new point with polar coordinates *r = 5* and *theta = π/4.*

Factory

Just like with Builder, we can take all the Point-creating functions out of Point and put them into a separate class that we call a Factory. It's actually very simple:

```
class PointFactory
{
  public static Point NewCartesianPoint(float x, float y)
  {
    return new Point(x, y); // needs to be public
  }
  // same for NewPolarPoint
}
```

It's worth noting that the Point constructor can no longer be private or protected because it needs to be externally accessible. Unlike C++, there is no friend keyword for us to use; we'll resort to a different trick later on.

For now, that's it: we have a dedicated class specifically designed for creating Point instances, to be used as follows:

```
var myPoint = PointFactory.NewCartesian(3, 4);
```

Inner Factory

An inner factory is simply a factory that is an inner (nested) class within the type it creates. Inner factories exist because inner classes can access the outer class's private members and, conversely, an outer class can access an inner class's private members. This means that our Point class can also be defined as follows:

```
public class Point
{
  // typical members here

  // note the constructor is again private
  private Point(double x, double y) { ... }

  public static class Factory
  {
    public static Point NewCartesianPoint(double x, double y)
    {
      return new Point(x, y); // using a private constructor
    }
    // similar for NewPolarPoint()
  }
}
```

Okay, so what is going on here? Well, we've stuck the Factory right into the class the Factory creates. This is convenient if a Factory only works with one single type, and not so convenient if a Factory relies on several types (and pretty much impossible if it needs their private members, too).

With this approach, we can now write

```
var point = Point.Factory.NewCartesianPoint(2, 3);
```

You might find this approach familiar because several parts of the .NET Framework use this approach to expose factories. For example, the Task-Parallel Library (TPL) lets you spin up new tasks with Task.Factory. StartNew().

Logical Separation

If you don't like the idea of having the entire definition of the Factory being placed into your Point.cs file, you can use the partial keyword because—guess what—it works on inner classes, too. First, in Point.cs, you would modify the Point type to now read

```
public partial class Point { ... }
```

Then, simply make a new file (e.g., Point.Factory.cs) and, inside it, define another part of Point; that is,

```
public partial class Point
{
  public static class Factory
  {
    // as before
  }
}
```

That's it! You have now physically separated the Factory from the type itself, even though logically they are still entwined because one contains the other.

Abstract Factory

So far, we have been looking at the construction of a single object. Sometimes, you might be involved in the creation of families of objects. This is actually a pretty rare case, so unlike Factory Method and the plain old Factory pattern, Abstract Factory is a pattern that only shows up in complicated systems. We need to talk about it, regardless, primarily for historical reasons.

Here is a simple scenario: suppose you are working at a café that serves tea and coffee. These two hot beverages are made through entirely different apparatus that we can both model as factories of sorts. Tea and coffee can actually be served both hot or cold, but let's focus on the hot variety. First of all, we can define an interface called IHotDrink:

```
public interface IHotDrink
{
  void Consume();
}
```

The Consume() is what we would call to consume the drink. For example, for a type Tea, it would be implemented as

```
internal class Tea : IHotDrink
{
  public void Consume()
  {
    Console.WriteLine("This tea is nice but I'd prefer it with
    milk.");
  }
}
```

And similarly for the Coffee type. Now, we could theorize that, for each type of beverage, we would require factories to implement some Prepare() method. The idea is that Prepare() makes a certain amount of a particular hot drink. Again, we leave its implementations to be rather trivial; for example:

```
internal class CoffeeFactory
{
  public IHotDrink Prepare(int amount)
  {
```

```
Console.WriteLine($"Grind some beans, boil water, pour
{amount} ml, add cream and sugar, enjoy!");
    return new Coffee();
  }
}
```

At this point, we could write a hypothetical MakeDrink() method that would take the name of a drink and make that drink. Given a discrete set of cases, it can look rather tedious:

```
public IHotDrink MakeDrink(string type)
{
  switch (type)
  {
    case "tea":
      return new TeaFactory().Prepare(200);
    case "coffee":
      return new CoffeeFactory().Prepare(50);
    default:
      throw new ArgumentException("type");
  }
}
```

Now, remember, different drinks are made by different machinery. In our case, we are interested in hot drinks, which we model through the aptly named IHotDrinkFactory interface:

```
public interface IHotDrinkFactory
{
  IHotDrink Prepare(int amount);
}
```

This type happens to be an Abstract Factory: it's a factory with a specific interface, but it's an abstract type, which means that even though it can feature as a function argument, for example, we would need concrete implementations to actually make the drinks. For example, in the case of making Coffee, we could write

```
internal class CoffeeFactory : IHotDrinkFactory
{
  public IHotDrink Prepare(int amount)
  {
    Console.WriteLine($"Grind some beans, boil water, pour
    {amount} ml, add cream and sugar, enjoy!");
    return new Coffee();
  }
}
```

The same goes for TeaFactory, as before. Now, suppose we want to define a higher-level interface for making different drinks, hot or cold. We could make a type called HotDrinkMachine that would itself contain references to the various factories that are available.

Functional Factory

Under the functional paradigm, the Factory pattern is of limited use, because F# prefers to work with concrete types whenever possible, using functions and functional composition to express variability in implementation.

If you wanted to go with interfaces (which F# allows), then, given the following definition

```
type ICountryInfo =
  abstract member Capital : string
```

```
type Country =
  | USA
  | UK
```

you could define a Factory function that, for a given country, yields a properly initialized ICountryInfo object:

```
let make country =
  match country with
  | USA -> { new ICountryInfo with
              member x.Capital = "Washington" }
  | UK -> { new ICountryInfo with
              member x.Capital = "London" }
```

Suppose you want to be able to create a country by specifying its name as a string. In this case, in addition to having a freestanding function that gives you the right Country type, you can have a static factory method very similar to the ones we have in the OOP world:

```
type Country =
  | USA
  | UK
with
  static member Create = function
    | "USA" | "America" -> USA
    | "UK" | "England" -> UK
    | _ -> failwith "No such country"

let usa = Country.Create "America"
```

Naturally, the Abstract Factory approach is similarly implementable using functional composition instead of inheritance.

Summary

Let's recap the terminology:

- A Factory Method is a class member that acts as a way of creating object. It typically replaces a constructor.

- A Factory is typically a separate class that knows how to construct objects, although if you pass a function (as in Func<T> or similar) that constructs objects, this argument is also called a factory.

- An Abstract Factory is, as its name suggests, an abstract class that can be inherited by concrete classes that offer a family of types. Abstract factories are rare in the wild.

A Factory has several critical advantages over a constructor call, namely these:

- A Factory can say *no*, meaning that instead of actually returning an object it can return, for example, a null or None of some Option<T> type.

- Naming is better and unconstrained, unlike constructor name.

- A single Factory can make objects of many different types.

- A Factory can exhibit polymorphic behavior, instantiating a class and returning it through a reference to its base class or interface.

- A Factory can implement caching and other storage optimizations; it is also a natural choice for approaches such as pooling or the Singleton pattern.

- A Factory can change its behavior at runtime; new is expected to always yield a new instance.

Factory is different from Builder in that, with a Factory, you typically create an object in one go (i.e., a single statement), whereas with Builder, you construct the object piecewise, either through several statements or, possibly, in a single statement if the Builder supports a fluent interface.

CHAPTER 5

Prototype

Think about something you use every day, like a car or a mobile phone. Chances are that it wasn't designed from scratch; instead, the manufacturer chose an existing design, made some improvements, made it visually distinctive from the old design (so people could show off) and started selling it, retiring the old product. It is a natural state of affairs, and in the software world, we have a similar situation: Sometimes, instead of creating an entire object from scratch (the Factory and Builder patterns can help here), you want to take a preconstructed object and either use a copy of it (which is easy) or, alternatively, customize it a little.

This leads us to the idea of having a Prototype, a model object that we can make copies of, customize, and then use them. The challenge of the Prototype pattern is really the copying part; everything else is easy.

Deep vs. Shallow Copying

Suppose we define a class Person as

```
public class Person
{
  public readonly string Name;
  public readonly Address Address;

  public Person(string name, Address address) { ... }
}
```

© Dmitri Nesteruk 2019
D. Nesteruk, *Design Patterns in .NET*, https://doi.org/10.1007/978-1-4842-4366-4_5

with the `Address` defined as

```
public class Address
{
  public readonly string StreetName;
  public int HouseNumber;

  public Address(string streetName, int houseNumber) { ... }
}
```

Suppose John Smith and Jane Smith are neighbors. It should be possible to construct John, then just copy him and change the house number, right? Well, using the assignment operator (=) certainly will not help:

```
var john = new Person(
  "John Smith",
  new Address("London Road", 123));

var jane = john;
jane.Name = "Jane Smith"; // John's name changed!
jane.Address.HouseNumber = 321; // John's address changed!
```

This does not work because now `john` and `jane` refer to the same object, so all changes to `jane` affect `john`, too. What we want is `jane` to become a new, independent object, whose modifications do not affect `john` in any way.

ICloneable Is Bad

The .NET Framework comes with an interface called `ICloneable`. This interface has a single method, `Clone()`, but this method is ill-specified: the documentation does not suggest whether this should be a shallow copy or a deep copy. Also, the name of the method, `Clone`, does not really help here because we don't know exactly what cloning does. The typical implementation of ICloneable for a type (say, Person) is something like this:

```
public class Person : ICloneable
{
  // members as before
  public Person Clone()
  {
    return (Person)MemberwiseClone();
  }
}
```

The method Object.MemberwiseClone() is a protected method of Object, so it is automatically inherited by every single reference type. It creates a *shallow copy* of the object. In other words, if you were to implement it on Address and Person in our example, you would run into the following problem:

```
var john = new Person(
  "John Smith",
  new Address("London Road", 123));

var jane = john.Clone();
jane.Name = "Jane Smith"; // John's name DID NOT change (good!)
jane.Address.HouseNumber = 321; // John's address changed :(
```

This helped, but not a lot. Even though the name is now assigned correctly, john and jane now share an Address reference—it was simply copied over, so they both point to the same Address. Shallow copy is therefore not for us: we want *deep copying*, recursive copying of all of an object's members and the construction of shiny new counterpart objects, each initialized with identical data.

Deep Copying with a Special Interface

If you want to have an interface specifically to indicate that your objects
support the notion of deep copying, I recommend you be explicit about it;
for example,

```
interface IDeepCopyable<T>
{
  T DeepCopy();
}
```

where T is the type of object to clone. Here is an example implementation:

```
public class Person : IDeepCopyable<Person>
{
  public string[] Names;
  public Address Address;

  public Person DeepCopy()
  {
    var copy = new Person();
    copy.Names = Array.Copy(Names);    // string[] is not
                                       //            IDeepCopyable
    copy.Address = Address.DeepCopy(); // Address is
                                       //            IDeepCopyable

    return copy;
  }
  // other members here
}
```

You'll notice that, in the implementation of DeepCopy(), we adopt
different strategies depending on whether or not the members are
themselves IDeepCopyable. If they are, things are fairly straightforward.

If they are not, we need to use an appropriate deep-copy mechanic for the given type. For example, for an array, you would call `Array.Copy()`.

This has two benefits compared to `ICloneable`:

- It is explicit in its intent: it talks specifically about deep copying.

- It is strongly typed, whereas `ICloneable` returns an `object` that you are expected to cast.

Deep Copying Objects

We are going to discuss how to perform deep copying of various fundamental .NET data types.

Value types such as `int`, `double`, and similar, as well as anything that is a `struct` (`DateTime`, `Guid`, `Decimal,` etc.) can be deep-copied using copy assignment:

```
var dt = new DateTime(2016, 1, 1);
var dt2 = dt; // deep copy!
```

The `string` type is a bit special: Even though it is a reference type, it is also immutable, meaning the value of a particular string cannot be changed. All we can do is reassign a *reference* that points to some string or another. The consequence is that, when deep-copying individual strings, we can continue to happily use the = operator:

```
string s = "hello";
string w = s; // w refers to "hello"
w = "world";  // w refers to "hello"
Console.WriteLine(s); // still prints "hello"
```

Then there are data structures you do not control. For example, arrays can be copied using `Array.Copy()`. To deep copy a `Dictionary<>`, you can use its copy constructor:

```
var d = new Dictionary<string, int>
{
  ["foo"] = 1,
  ["bar"] = 2
};
var d2 = new Dictionary<string, int>(d);
d2["foo"] = 55;
Console.WriteLine(d["foo"]); // prints 1
```

Even a structure such as a `Dictionary`, however, has no idea how to deep copy reference types it contains, so if you try to use this approach to deep copy a `Dictionary<string, Address>`, you're going to be out of luck:

```
var d = new Dictionary<string, Address>
{
  ["sherlock"] = new Address {HouseNumber = 221, StreetName =
  "Baker St"}
};
var d2 = new Dictionary<string, Address>(d);
d2["sherlock"].HouseNumber = 222;
Console.WriteLine(d["sherlock"].HouseNumber); // prints "222"
```

Instead, you have to make sure that deep copying is performed on each value of the dictionary; for example:

```
var d2 = d.ToDictionary(x => x.Key, x => x.Value.DeepCopy());
```

The same goes for other collections: `Array.Copy` is fine if you are storing strings or integers, but for composite objects, it just won't do. This is where LINQ's various collection-generating operations, such as `ToArray()`/`ToList()`/`ToDictionary()`, are very useful.

Duplication via Copy Construction

The simplest way of implementing proper duplication is to implement *copy constructors*. A copy constructor is an artifact straight from the C++ world—it is a constructor that takes another instance of the type we are in and copies that type into the current object; for example:

```
public Address(Address other)
{
  StreetAddress = other.StreetAddress;
  City = other.City;
  Country = other.Country;
}
```

And, similarly

```
public Person(Person other)
{
  Name = other.Name;
  Address = new Address(other.Address); // uses a copy
  constructor here
}
```

This allows us to perform a deep copy of john to jane:

```
var john = new Person(
  "John Smith",
  new Address("London Road", 123));

var jane = new Person(john); // copy constructor!
jane.Name = "Jane Smith";
jane.Address.HouseNumber = 321; // john is still at 123
```

You'll notice that, although strings are reference types, we do not have to perform any action to deep copy them. This is because strings are immutable, and you cannot actually modify a string, only construct a new string and rebind the references. That means one less thing to worry about.

Beware, though. If, for example, we had an *array* of names (i.e., `string [] names`), we would have to explicitly copy the entire array using `Array.Copy` because arrays are mutable. The same goes for any other data type that isn't a primitive type, `string,` or a `struct`.

Now, the copy constructor is pretty good in that it provides a unified copying interface, but it is of little help if the client is unable to discover it. At least when developers see an `IDeepCopyable` interface with a `DeepCopy()` method, they know what they are getting; discoverability of a copy constructor is suspect. Another problem with this approach is that it is very intrusive: It requires that every single class in the composition chain implement a copy constructor, and will likely malfunction if any class does not do it correctly. As such, it's a very challenging approach to use on preexisting data structures, as you would be violating OCP on a massive scale if you wanted to support this post-hoc.

Serialization

We need to thank the designers of C# for the fact that most objects in C#, whether they be primitive types or collections, are 'trivially serializable': by default, you should be able take a class and save it to a file or to memory without adding extra code to the class (well, maybe an attribute or two, at most) or fiddling with reflection.

Why is this relevant to the problem at hand? If you can serialize something to a file or to memory, you can then deserialize it, preserving all the information, including all the dependent objects. Isn't this convenient? For example, you could define an extension method for in-memory cloning using binary serialization:

```
public static T DeepCopy<T>(this T self)
{
  using (var stream = new MemoryStream())
  {
    BinaryFormatter formatter = new BinaryFormatter();
    formatter.Serialize(stream, self);
    stream.Seek(0, SeekOrigin.Begin);
    object copy = formatter.Deserialize(stream);
    return (T) copy;
  }
}
```

This code simply takes an object of any type T, performs binary serialization into memory, and then deserializes from that memory, thereby gaining a deep copy of the original object.

This approach is fairly universal, and will let you easily clone your objects:

```
var foo = new Foo { Stuff = 42, Whatever = new Bar { Baz =
"abc"} };
var foo2 = foo.DeepCopy();
foo2.Whatever.Baz = "xyz"; // works fine
```

There is just one catch: Binary serialization requires every class to be marked with [Serializable], otherwise the serializer simply throws an exception (not a good thing). So, if we wanted to use this approach on an existing set of classes, we might go with a different approach that doesn't require the aforementioned attribute. For example, you could use Extensible Markup Language (XML) serialization instead:

```
public static T DeepCopyXml<T>(this T self)
{
  using (var ms = new MemoryStream())
  {
```

```
    XmlSerializer s = new XmlSerializer(typeof(T));
    s.Serialize(ms, self);
    ms.Position = 0;
    return (T) s.Deserialize(ms);
  }
}
```

You can use any serializer you want; the only requirement is that it knows how to traverse every single element in the object graph. Most serializers are smart enough to go over things that shouldn't be serialized (like read-only properties), but sometimes they need a little help to make sense of trickier structures. That's what all those attributes are actually for.

Prototype Factory

If you have predefined objects that you want to replicate, where do you actually store them? A global variable? Perhaps. In fact, suppose our company has both main and auxiliary offices. Now we could try to declare some static variables; for example:

```
static Person main = new Person(null,
  new Address("123 East Dr", "London", 0));
static Person aux = new Person(null,
  new Address("123B East Dr", "London", 0));
```

We could stick these members into Person so as to provide a hint that, when you need a person working at a main office, just clone main, and similarly for the auxiliary office, one could clone aux. This is far from intuitive, though: what if we want to prohibit construction of people working anywhere other than these two offices? From the SRP perspective, it would also make sense to keep the set of possible addresses separate.

This is where a Prototype Factory comes into play. Just like an ordinary factory, it can store these static members and provide convenience methods for creating new employees:

```
public class EmployeeFactory
{
  private static Person main =
    new Person(null, new Address("123 East Dr", "London", 0));
  private static Person aux =
    new Person(null, new Address("123B East Dr", "London", 0));

  public static Person NewMainOfficeEmployee(string name, int
  suite) =>
    NewEmployee(main, name, suite);

  public static Person NewAuxOfficeEmployee(string name, int
  suite) =>
    NewEmployee(aux, name, suite);

  private static Person NewEmployee(Person proto, string name,
  int suite)
  {
    var copy = proto.DeepCopy();
    copy.Name = name;
    copy.Address.Suite = suite;
    return copy;
  }
}
```

Notice how, following the DRY principle, we don't call DeepCopy() in more than one location: all the different NewXxxEmployee() methods simply forward their arguments to one private NewEmployee() method, passing it the prototype to use when constructing a new object.

The preceding Prototype Factory can now be used as:

```
var john = EmployeeFactory.NewMainOfficeEmployee("John Doe", 100);
var jane = EmployeeFactory.NewAuxOfficeEmployee("Jane Doe", 123);
```

Naturally, this implementation assumes that the constructors of Person are accessible; if you want to keep them private or protected, you'll need to implement the Inner Factory approach as outlined in Chapter 4.

Summary

The Prototype design pattern embodies the notion of deep copying of objects so that, instead of doing full initialization each time, you can take a premade object, copy it, fiddle with it a little bit, and then use it independently of the original.

There are really only two ways of implementing the Prototype pattern. They are:

- Writing code that correctly duplicates your object; that is, performs a deep copy. This can be done in a copy constructor, or you can define an appropriately named method, possibly with a corresponding interface (but not ICloneable).

- Writing code for the support of serialization and deserialization and then use this mechanism to implement cloning as serialization immediately followed by deserialization. This carries an extra computational cost; its impact depends on how often you need to do the copying. The advantage of this approach is that you can get away without significantly modifying existing structures. It is also much safer, because you are less likely to forget to clone a member properly.

Don't forget that for value types, the cloning problem does not really exist: if you want to clone a `struct`, just assign it to a new variable. Also, strings are immutable, so you can use the assignment operator = on them without worrying that subsequent modification will affect more objects than it should.

CHAPTER 6

Singleton

> When discussing which patterns to drop, we found that we still love them all. (Not really—I'm in favor of dropping Singleton. Its use is almost always a design smell.)
>
> —Erich Gamma

The Singleton is the most hated design pattern in the (rather limited) history of design patterns. That said, however, it doesn't mean you shouldn't use the Singleton: a toilet brush is not the most pleasant device either, but sometimes it is simply necessary.

The Singleton design pattern grew out of a very simple idea that you should only have one instance of a particular component in your application. For example, a component that loads a database into memory and offers a read-only interface is a prime candidate for a Singleton because it really doesn't make sense to waste memory storing several identical datasets. In fact, your application might have constraints such that two or more instances of the database simply won't fit into memory, or will result in such a lack of memory as to cause the program to malfunction.

© Dmitri Nesteruk 2019
D. Nesteruk, *Design Patterns in .NET*, https://doi.org/10.1007/978-1-4842-4366-4_6

Singleton by Convention

The naïve approach to this problem is to simply agree that we are not going to instantiate this object more than once; that is:

```
public class Database
{
  /// <summary>
  /// Please do not create more than one instance.
  /// </summary>
  public Database() {}
};
```

The problem with this approach, apart from the fact that your developer colleagues might simply ignore the advice, is that objects can be created in stealthy ways where the call to the constructor is not immediately obvious. This can be anything—a call through reflection, creation in a factory (e.g., `Activator.CreateInstance`), or injection of the type by an inversion of control (IoC) container.

The most obvious idea that comes to mind is to offer a single, static global object:

```
public static class Globals
{
  public static Database Database = new Database();
}
```

This really doesn't do much in terms of safety, though: Clients are not in any way prevented from constructing additional Databases as they see fit. In addition, how will the client find the Globals class?

Classic Implementation

Now that we know what the problem is, how can we turn life sour for those interested in making more than one instance of an object? Simply put a static counter right in the constructor and throw if the value is ever incremented:

```
public class Database
{
  private static int instanceCount = 0;
  Database()
  {
    if (++instanceCount > 1)
      throw new InvalidOperationException("Cannot make >1
      database!");
  }
};
```

This is a particularly hostile approach to the problem: even though it prevents the creation of more than one instance by throwing an exception, it fails to communicate the fact that we do not want anyone calling the constructor more than once. Even if you adorn it with plenty of XML documentation, I guarantee there will still be some poor soul trying to call this more than once in some nondeterminstic setting, and probably in production, too!

The only way to prevent explicit construction of Database is to make its constructor private and introduce a property or method to return the one and only instance:

```
public class Database
{
  private Database() { ... }
  public static Database Instance { get; } = new Database();
}
```

93

Note how we removed the possibility of directly creating Database instances by hiding the constructor. Of course, you can use reflection to access private members, so construction of this class isn't quite impossible, but it does require extra hoops to jump through, and hopefully this is enough to prevent most people from trying to construct one.

By declaring the instance as static, we removed any possibility of controlling the lifetime of the database: It now lives as long as the program does.

Lazy Loading

The implementation shown in the previous section happens to be thread-safe. After all, static constructors are guaranteed to run only once per AppDomain, before any instances of the class are created or any static members accessed.

What if you don't want initialization in the static constructor, though? What if, instead, you want to initialize the Singleton (i.e., call its constructor) only when the object is first accessed? In this case, you can use Lazy<T>:[1]

```
public class MyDatabase
{
  private MyDatabase()
  {
    Console.WriteLine("Initializing database");
  }
  private static Lazy<MyDatabase> instance =
    new Lazy<MyDatabase>(() => new MyDatabase());

  public static MyDatabase Instance => instance.Value;
}
```

---

[1]Note that, similar to C#, F#'s default implementation also uses lazy. The only difference is that F# has a somewhat more concise syntax: writing lazy(x + y()) automatically constructs a Lazy<'T> behind the scenes.

This is also a thread-safe approach because the objects Lazy<T> creates are thread-safe by default. In a multithreaded setting, the first thread to access the Value property of a Lazy<T> is the one that initializes it for all subsequent accesses on all threads.

The Trouble with Singleton

Let us now consider a concrete example of a Singleton. Suppose that our database contains a list of capital cities and their populations. The interface that our Singleton database is going to conform to is:

```
public interface IDatabase
{
  int GetPopulation(string name);
}
```

We have a single method that gives us the population of a given city. Now, let us suppose that this interface is adopted by a concrete implementation called SingletonDatabase that implements the Singleton the same way as we have done before:

```
public class SingletonDatabase : IDatabase
{
  private Dictionary<string, int> capitals;
  private static int instanceCount;
  public static int Count => instanceCount;

  private SingletonDatabase()
  {
    WriteLine("Initializing database");

    capitals = File.ReadAllLines(
      Path.Combine(
```

```
      new FileInfo(typeof(IDatabase).Assembly.Location).
      DirectoryName,
        "capitals.txt")
    )
    .Batch(2) // from MoreLINQ
    .ToDictionary(
      list => list.ElementAt(0).Trim(),
      list => int.Parse(list.ElementAt(1)));
  }

  public int GetPopulation(string name)
  {
    return capitals[name];
  }

  private static Lazy<SingletonDatabase> instance =
    new Lazy<SingletonDatabase>(() =>
    {
      instanceCount++;
      return new SingletonDatabase();
    });

  public static IDatabase Instance => instance.Value;
}
```

The constructor of the database reads the names and populations of various capitals from a text file and stores them in a Dictionary<>. The GetPopulation() method is used as an accessor to get the population of a given city.

As we noted before, the real problem with Singletons like the one given is their use in other components. Here's what I mean: suppose that, on the basis of what we just showed, we build a component for calculating the sum total population of several different cities:

```
public class SingletonRecordFinder
{
  public int TotalPopulation(IEnumerable<string> names)
  {
    int result = 0;
    foreach (var name in names)
      result += SingletonDatabase.Instance.GetPopulation(name);
    return result;
  }
}
```

The trouble is that SingletonRecordFinder is now firmly dependent on SingletonDatabase. This presents an issue for testing: if we want to check that SingletonRecordFinder works correctly, we need to use data from the actual database; that is:

```
[Test]
public void SingletonTotalPopulationTest()
{
  // testing on a live database
  var rf = new SingletonRecordFinder();
  var names = new[] {"Seoul", "Mexico City"};
  int tp = rf.TotalPopulation(names);
  Assert.That(tp, Is.EqualTo(17500000 + 17400000));
}
```

This is a terrible unit test. It tries to read a live database (something that you typically do not want to do too often), but it is also very fragile, because it depends on the concrete values in the database. What if the population of Seoul changes (as a result of North Korea opening its borders, perhaps)? Then the test will break. Of course, many people run tests on Continuous Integration (CI) systems that are isolated from live databases, so that fact makes the approach even more dubious.

This test is also bad for ideological reasons. Remember, we want a *unit* test where the unit we are testing is the SingletonRecordFinder. However, the test just shown is not a unit test, but an *integration* test because the record finder uses SingletonDatabase, so in effect we're testing both systems at the same time. There is nothing wrong with that if an integration test is what you wanted, but we would really prefer to test the record finder in isolation.

Now we know we don't want to use an actual database in a test. Can we replace the database with some dummy component that we can control from within our tests? Well, in our current design, this is impossible, and it is precisely this inflexibility that is the Singeton's downfall.

What can we do, then? Well, for one, we need to stop depending on SingletonDatabase explicitly. Because all we need is something implementing the Database interface, we can create a new ConfigurableRecordFinder that lets us configure where the data comes from:

```
public class ConfigurableRecordFinder
{
  private IDatabase database;

  public ConfigurableRecordFinder(IDatabase database)
  {
    this.database = database;
  }

  public int GetTotalPopulation(IEnumerable<string> names)
  {
    int result = 0;
    foreach (var name in names)
      result += database.GetPopulation(name);
    return result;
  }
}
```

We now use the database reference instead of using the Singleton explicitly. This lets us make a dummy database specifically for testing the record finder:

```
public class DummyDatabase : IDatabase
{
  public int GetPopulation(string name)
  {
    return new Dictionary<string, int>
    {
      ["alpha"] = 1,
      ["beta"] = 2,
      ["gamma"] = 3
    }[name];
  }
}
```

Now, we can rewrite our unit test to take advantage of this DummyDatabase:

```
[Test]
public void DependentTotalPopulationTest()
{
  var db = new DummyDatabase();
  var rf = new ConfigurableRecordFinder(db);
  Assert.That(
    rf.GetTotalPopulation(new[]{"alpha", "gamma"}),
    Is.EqualTo(4));
}
```

This test is more robust because if data changes in the actual database, we won't have to adjust our unit test values—the dummy data stays the same. Also, it opens interesting possibilities. We can now run tests against an empty database or, say, a database whose size is greater than the available RAM. You get the idea.

Singletons and Inversion of Control

The approach with explicitly making a component a Singleton is distinctly invasive, and a decision to stop treating the class as a Singleton down the line will end up being particularly costly. An alternative solution is to adopt a convention where, instead of directly enforcing the lifetime of a class, this function is outsourced to an Inversion of Control (IoC) container.

Here's what defining a Singleton component looks like when using the Autofac dependency injection (DI) framework:

```
var builder = new ContainerBuilder();
builder.RegisterType<Database>().SingleInstance(); // <-- singleton!
builder.RegisterType<RecordFinder>();

var container = builder.Build();
var finder = container.Resolve<RecordFinder>();
var finder2 = container.Resolve<RecordFinder>();
WriteLine(ReferenceEquals(finder, finder2)); // True
// finder and finder2 refer to the same database
```

Many people believe that using a Singleton in a DI container is the only socially acceptable use of a Singleton. At least with this approach, if you need to replace a Singleton object with something else, you can do it in one central place: the container configuration code. An added benefit is that you won't have to implement any Singleton logic yourself, which prevents possible errors. Oh, and did I mention that all container operations in Autofac are thread-safe?

In actual fact, one thing IoC containers highlight is the fact that a Singleton is only a unique case of lifetime management (one object per lifetime of the entire application). Different lifetimes are possible—you can have one object per thread, one object per web request, and so on. You can also have *pooling*—situations where the number of live object instances can be between 0 and X, whatever X happens to be.

Monostate

Monostate is a variation on the Singleton pattern. It is a class that behaves like a Singleton while appearing as an ordinary class.

For example, suppose you are modeling a company structure, and a company typically has only one CEO. You can define the following class:

```
public class ChiefExecutiveOfficer
{
  private static string name;
  private static int age;

  public string Name
  {
    get => name;
    set => name = value;
  }

  public int Age
  {
    get => age;
    set => age = value;
  }
}
```

Can you see what is happening here? The class appears as an ordinary class with getters and setters, but they actually work on static data!

This might seem like a really neat trick: you let people instantiate ChiefExecutiveOfficer as many times as they want, but all the instances refer to the same data. How are users supposed to know this, though? A user will happily instantiate two CEOs, assign them different ids, and be very surprised when both of them are identical!

The Monostate approach works to some degree and has a couple of advantages. For example, it is easy to inherit, it can leverage polymorphism, and its lifetime is reasonbly well-defined (but then again, you might not always wish it so). Its greatest advantage is that you can take an existing object that is already used throughout the system, patch it up to behave in a Monostate way, and provided your system works fine with the nonplurality of object intances, you've got yourself a Singleton-like implementation with no extra code needing to be rewritten.

That's all that Monostate really is: a bandage when you want one component to become a Singleton throughout the entire code base without any large-scale changes. This pattern is not meant for production, as it can cause too much confusion. If you need centralized control over things, a DI container is your best bet.

Summary

Singletons are not totally evil but, when used carelessly, they will mess up the testability and refactorability of your application. If you really must use a Singleton, try to avoid using it directly (as in, writing `SomeComponent.Instance.Foo()`) and instead keep specifying it as a dependency (e.g., a constructor argument) where all dependencies are satisfied from a single location in your application (e.g., an IoC container).

PART III

Structural Patterns

As the name suggests, structural patterns are all about setting up the structure of your application so as to improve SOLID conformance as well as general usability and maintainability of your code.

When it comes to determining the structure of an object, we can apply three fairly well-known methods:

- *Inheritance*: an object automagically acquires all members of the base class or classes. To allow instantiation, the object must implement every abstract member from its parent; if it does not, it is abstract and cannot be created (but you can inherit from it).

- *Composition*: This generally implies that the child cannot exist without the parent. This is typically implemented with nested classes. For example, a class `Car` can have a nested class `Wheel`.

- *Aggregation*: An object can contain another object, but that object can also exist independently. Think of a `Car` having a `Person driver` field or property.

Nowadays, both composition and aggregation are treated in an identical fashion. If you have a `Person` class with a field of type `Address`, you have a choice as to whether `Address` is an external type or a nested type. In either case, provided it's `public`, you can instantiate it as either `Address` or `Person.Address`.

I would argue that using the word *composition* when we really mean aggregation has become so commonplace that we might as well use them in interchangeable fashion. Here's some proof: when we talk about IoC containers, we speak of a *composition root*. But doesn't the IoC container control the lifetime of each object individually? It does, so we're using the word *composition* when we really mean *aggregation.*

There are, fundamentally, three ways in which data structures can be defined in C#:

- *Statically*, when you simply write the classes and they get compiled. This is the most common case out there.

- *Via code generation.* This happens when structures get created from T4 templates or databases or some user scripts. Plenty of code gets generated behind the scenes when you edit UI, (e.g., in a WinForms or WPF application).

- *Dynamically*, i.e., at runtime. This is the most sophisticated option. Advanced libraries are capable of constructing data structures and compiling them into executable code right at the moment when the application is executing. This approach is sometimes leveraged in design patterns and gives rise to their static–dynamic duality.

CHAPTER 7

Adapter

I used to travel quite a lot, and a travel adapter that lets me plug a European plug into a UK or U.S. socket[1] is a very good analogy for what's going on with the Adapter pattern: we are given an interface, but we want a different one, and building an adapter over the interface is what gets us to where we want to be.

Scenario

Here's a trivial example: suppose you are working with a library that's great at drawing pixels. You, on the other hand, work with geometric objects—lines, rectangles, and that sort of thing. You want to keep working with those objects, but also need the rendering, so you need to *adapt* your vector geometry to pixel-based representation.

Let us begin by defining the (rather simple) domain objects of our example:

```
public class Point
{
  public int X, Y;
  // other members omitted
}
```

---

[1]Just in case you're European like me and want to complain that everyone should be using European plugs and sockets, the UK plug design is technically better and safer, so if we did want just one standard, the UK one would be the one to use.

© Dmitri Nesteruk 2019
D. Nesteruk, *Design Patterns in .NET*, https://doi.org/10.1007/978-1-4842-4366-4_7

```
public class Line
{
  public Point Start, End;
  // other members omitted
}
```

Let's now theorize about vector geometry. A typical vector object is likely to be defined by a collection of Line objects. Thus, we can make a class that would simply inherit from Collection<Line>:

```
public abstract class VectorObject : Collection<Line> {}
```

This way, if you want to define, say, a Rectangle, you can simply inherit from this type and there's no need to define additional storage:

```
public class VectorRectangle : VectorObject
{
  public VectorRectangle(int x, int y, int width, int height)
  {
    Add(new Line(new Point(x,y), new Point(x+width, y) ));
    Add(new Line(new Point(x+width,y), new Point(x+width,
    y+height) ));
    Add(new Line(new Point(x,y), new Point(x, y+height) ));
    Add(new Line(new Point(x,y+height), new Point(x+width,
    y+height) ));
  }
}
```

Now, here's the setup. Suppose we want to draw lines on screen, or rectangles, even! Unfortunately, we cannot, because the only interface for drawing is literally this:

```
// the interface we have
public static void DrawPoint(Point p)
{
```

```
  bitmap.SetPixel(p.X, p.Y, Color.Black);
}
```

I am using the Bitmap class here for illustration, but the actual implementation doesn't matter. Let's just take this at face value: We only have an API for drawing pixels. That's it.

Adapter

Suppose we want to draw a couple of rectangles:

```
private static readonly List<VectorObject> vectorObjects
  = new List<VectorObject>
{
  new VectorRectangle(1, 1, 10, 10),
  new VectorRectangle(3, 3, 6, 6)
};
```

To draw these objects, we need to convert every one of them from a series of lines into a rather large number of points. For this, we make a separate class that will store the points and expose them as a collection. This is our Adapter pattern!

```
public class LineToPointAdapter : Collection<Point>
{
  private static int count = 0;

  public LineToPointAdapter(Line line)
  {
    WriteLine($"{++count}: Generating points for line"
        + $" [{line.Start.X},{line.Start.Y}]-"
        + $"[{line.End.X},{line.End.Y}] (no caching)");

    int left = Math.Min(line.Start.X, line.End.X);
    int right = Math.Max(line.Start.X, line.End.X);
```

```
  int top = Math.Min(line.Start.Y, line.End.Y);
  int bottom = Math.Max(line.Start.Y, line.End.Y);

  if (right - left == 0)
  {
    for (int y = top; y <= bottom; ++y)
    {
      Add(new Point(left, y));
    }
  } else if (line.End.Y - line.Start.Y == 0)
  {
    for (int x = left; x <= right; ++x)
    {
      Add(new Point(x, top));
    }
  }
  }
}
```

This is trivial: we only handle perfectly vertical or horizontal lines and ignore everything else. The conversion from a line to a number of points happens right in the constructor, so our adapter is eager; don't worry, we'll make it lazy toward the end of this chapter.

We can now use this adapter to actually render some objects. We take the two rectangles from earlier and simply render them like this:

```
private static void DrawPoints()
{
  foreach (var vo in vectorObjects)
  {
    foreach (var line in vo)
    {
      var adapter = new LineToPointAdapter(line);
```

```
      adapter.ForEach(DrawPoint);
    }
  }
}
```

Beautiful! All we do is, for every vector object, get each of its lines, construct a `LineToPointAdapter` for that line, and then iterate the set of points produced by the adapter, feeding them to `DrawPoint()`. It works (trust me, it does).

Adapter Temporaries

There is a major problem with our code, though: `DrawPoints()` gets called on literally every screen refresh that we might need, which means the same data for the same line objects gets regenerated by the adapter far too many times. What can we do about it?

Well, on one hand, we can make some lazy-loading method; for example:

```
private static List<Point> points = new List<Point>();
private static bool prepared = false;

private static void Prepare()
{
  if (prepared) return;
  foreach (var vo in vectorObjects)
  {
    foreach (var line in vo)
    {
      var adapter = new LineToPointAdapter(line);
      adapter.ForEach(p => points.Add(p));
    }
  }
}
```

```
  prepared = true;
}
```

Then the implementation of DrawPoints() simplifies to

```
private static void DrawPointsLazy()
{
  Prepare();
  points.ForEach(DrawPoint);
}
```

Let's suppose, for a moment though, that the original set of vectorObjects can change. Saving those points forever makes no sense then, but we still want to avoid the incessant regeneration of potentially repeating data. How do we deal with this? With caching, of course!

First of all, to avoid regeneration, we need unique ways of identifying lines, which transitively means we need unique ways of identifying points. ReSharper's **Generate | Equality Members** to the rescue:

```
public class Point
{
  // other members here

  protected bool Equals(Point other) { ... }
  public override bool Equals(object obj) { ... }

  public override int GetHashCode()
  {
    unchecked { return (X * 397) ^ Y; }
  }
}

public class Line
{
  // other members here
```

```csharp
protected bool Equals(Line other) { ... }
public override bool Equals(object obj) { ... }

public override int GetHashCode()
{
  unchecked
  {
    return ((Start != null ? Start.GetHashCode() : 0) * 397)
      ^ (End != null ? End.GetHashCode() : 0);
  }
}
}
```

As you can see, ReSharper (or Rider, if you prefer that IDE) has generated different implementations of Equals() as well as GetHashCode(). The latter is more important because it allows us to uniquely (to some degree) identify an object by its hash code without peforming a direct comparison. Now, we can build a new LineToPointCachingAdapter such that it caches the points and regenerates them only when necessary; that is, when their hashes differ. The implementation is almost the same except for the following nuances.

First, the adapter now has a static cache of points that correspond to particular lines:

```csharp
static Dictionary<int, List<Point>> cache
  = new Dictionary<int, List<Point>>();
```

The type int here is precisely the type returned from GetHashCode(). Now, when processing a Line in the constructor, we first check whether or not the line is already cached: If it is, we don't need to do anything:

```csharp
hash = line.GetHashCode();
if (cache.ContainsKey(hash)) return; // we already have it
```

Notice that we actually store the hash of the current adapter in its nonstatic field. This allows us to store and use adapters that correspond to individual lines. Alternatively, we could make the entire adapter static.

The full implementation of the constructor is as before, except that instead of calling Add() for the generated points, we simply add them to the cache:

```
public LineToPointAdapter(Line line)
{
  hash = line.GetHashCode();
  if (cache.ContainsKey(hash)) return; // we already have it

  List<Point> points = new List<Point>();

  // points are added to the 'points' member as before, then...

  cache.Add(hash, points);
}
```

Finally, we need to implement IEnumerable<Point>. This is easy: We use the hash field to reach into the cache and yield the right set of points:

```
public IEnumerator<Point> GetEnumerator()
{
  return cache[hash].GetEnumerator();
}
```

Thanks to hash functions and caching, we have drastically cut down on the number of conversions being made. The only issue with this implementation is that, in a long-running program, the cache can accumulate a huge number of unnecessary point collections. How would you clean it up? One idea would be to set up a timer to wipe the entire cache at regular intervals. See if you can come up with other possible solutions to this problem.

The Problem with Hashing

One reason we implemented the adapter the way we did is that our current implementation is robust with respect to changes in objects. If any aspect of a Rectangle changes, the adapter will calculate a different hash value and will regenerate the appropriate set of points.

This is effectively done by *polling*: any time an adapted dataset is required, we take the target object and recalculate its hash. The assumption is always that the hash can be calculated quickly, and that hash collisions—situations where two different objects have identical hashes—are unlikely. Let's remind ourselves of how Point hashes are calculated:

```
public override int GetHashCode()
{
  unchecked
  {
    return (X * 397) ^ Y;
  }
}
```

The truth is, the hash function for a Point is a pretty bad hash function and will give us lots of collisions. For example, points (0,0) and (1, 397) will give the same hash value of 0, which means, in turn, that two lines with these Start points and an identical End point will end up overwriting each other's generated set of points with incorrect data, inevitably causing problems.

How would you solve this issue? Well, you could pick a prime number N that is larger than 397. That way, if you can guarantee that your values are less than this larger N, you won't have any collisions. Alternatively, you could go for a more robust hashing function. In the case of a Point, assuming positive X and Y, this could be as simple as

```
public long MyHashFunction()
{
  return (X << 32) | Y;
}
```

If you really wanted to preserve the GetHashCode() interface (it returns an int, remember), you could do it by downgrading the coordinates to a short—its range is plenty for a screen coordinate. Finally, there are many sophisticated functions out there (Cantor pairing function, Szudzik function, etc.) that are able to handle situations at the boundaries of the range of numbers.

The point I am trying to make here is that the calculation of hashing functions is a slippery slope: the code generated by IDEs might not be as robust as you think. What can we do to avoid all of this? We can hold a reference to the adaptee, rather than the hash, in our cache. It's as simple as this:

```
public class LineToPointAdapter
  : IEnumerable<Point>
{
  static Dictionary<Line, List<Point>> cache
    = new Dictionary<Line, List<Point>>();
  private Line line;

  public LineToPointAdapter(Line line)
  {
    if (cache.ContainsKey(line)) return; // we already have it
    this.line = line;

    // as before

    cache.Add(line, points);
  }
```

```
public IEnumerator<Point> GetEnumerator()
{
  return cache[line].GetEnumerator();
}
}
```

What's the difference? Well, the difference is that, when searching through the dictionary, both GetHashCode() and Equals() are used to find the right item. As a result, collisions can still occur, but they won't mess up the final value. This approach does have its downsides though; for example, the lifetime of lines is now bound to the adapter because it has strong references to them.

This approach of holding on to the reference gives us an additional benefit: laziness. Instead of calculating everything in the constructor, we can split the preparation of points into a separate function that only gets invoked when adapter points are iterated:

```
public class LineToPointAdapter : IEnumerable<Point>
{
  ...
  private void Prepare()
  {
    if (cache.ContainsKey(line)) return; // we already have it
    // rest of code as before
  }

  public IEnumerator<Point> GetEnumerator()
  {
    Prepare();
    return cache[line].GetEnumerator();
  }
}
```

Property Adapter (Surrogate)

One very common application of the Adapter design pattern is to get your class to provide additional properties that serve only one purpose: to take existing fields or properties and expose them in some useful way, quite often as projections to a different data type.

Consider the following example: If you have an IDictionary member, you cannot use an XmlSerializer because Microsoft did not implement this functionality "due to schedule constraints." Consequently, if you want a serializable dictionary, you have two options: you either go online and search for a SerializableDictionary implementation or, alternatively, you build a property adapter (or surrogate) that exposes the dictionary in a way that is easy to serialize.

For example, suppose you need to serialize the following property:

```
public Dictionary<string, string> Capitals { get; set; }
```

To make it happen, you would first mark the property as [XmlIgnore]. You would then construct another property of a type that can be serialized, such as an array of tuples:

```
public (string, string)[] CapitalsSerializable
{
  get
  {
    return Capitals.Keys.Select(country =>
      (country, Capitals[country])).ToArray();
  }
  set
  {
    Capitals = value.ToDictionary(x => x.Item1, x => x.Item2);
  }
}
```

I have made a very careful choice of types for serialization here:

- The overall type of the variable is an array. If you made this a List, the serializer would never call the setter, and would instead try to use the getter and then Add() to that getter—we definitely don't want that.

- We are using a ValueTuple instead of an ordinary Tuple. Conventional tuples cannot be serialized because they do not have parameterless constructors, whereas ValueTuples do not have this problem.

In case you are wondering, here's how a serialized class would look in XML:

```xml
<?xml version="1.0" encoding="utf-16"?>
<CountryStats xmlns:xsi="http://www.w3.org/2001/XMLSchema-instance"
  xmlns:xsd="http://www.w3.org/2001/XMLSchema">
  <CapitalsSerializable>
    <ValueTupleOfStringString>
      <Item1>France</Item1>
      <Item2>Paris</Item2>
    </ValueTupleOfStringString>
  </CapitalsSerializable>
</CountryStats>
```

The adapter presented here is quite different from what you might expect because the API we are trying to adapt the class to is *implicit*—serialization mechanics are concealed by the serializer we are using, so the only way to know about this issue is through trial and error.[2]

---

[2]You really want to use third-party serialization components if you can. The support for both binary and XML serialization in .NET is very patchy and has lots of unpleasant caveats. If you were to take a JSON serializer such as JSON.NET, none of the problems described here would be an issue.

This example is a bit ambiguous with respect to SOLID principles: on the one hand, we're separating out the serialization concern. On the other hand, should this really be part of the class itself? It would be a lot neater if we could decorate the member with some [SerializeThisDictionary] attribute and have the conversion process handled elsewhere. Alas, such are the limitations of the way serialization is implemented in .NET.

Adapters in the .NET Framework

There are many uses of the Adapter pattern in the .NET Framework, including these:

- ADO.NET providers living in System.Data, such as SqlCommand, adapt an OOP-defined database command or query to be executed using SQL. Each ADO.NET provider is an adapter for a particular database type.

- Database data adapters—types that inherit from DbDataAdapter—perform a similar, higher level operation. Internally, they represent a set of data commands and a connection to a particular data source (a database, typically), their goal being to populate a DataSet and update the data source.

- LINQ providers are also adapters, each adapting some underlying storage technology to be usable through LINQ operators (Select, Where, etc.). Expression trees exist with the central purpose of translating conventional C# lambda functions into other query languages and mechanisms such as SQL.

- Stream adapters (e.g., `TextReader`, `StreamWriter`) adapt a stream to read a particular type of data (binary, text) into a particular type of object. For example, a `StringWriter` writes into a buffer held by a `StringBuilder`.

- WPF uses the `IValueConverter` interface to allow scenarios such as a text field being bound to a numeric value. Unlike most of the adapters here, this one is *bidirectional*, meaning that the interface is adapted in both directions: Changes to a numeric field or property get turned into text displayed in the control and, conversely, text entered into the control gets parsed and converted into a numeric value.

- Interop-related entities in C# represent the Adapter pattern. For example, that dummy P/Invoke type that you write allows you to adapt a C/C++ library to your C# needs. The same goes for runtime-callable wrappers (RCWs), which allow managed classes and COM components to interact despite their obvious interface differences.

Summary

Adapter is a very simple concept: it allows you to adapt the interface you have to the interface you need. The only real issue with Adapters is that, in the process of adaptation, you sometimes end up generating temporary data to satisfy requirements related to representation of data in a form palatable for the target API. When this happens, we turn to caching, ensuring that new data is only generated when necessary. If we are implementing caching with a special key, we need to ensure that collisions are either impossible or are handled appropriately. If we are using the object itself as the underlying key, the presence of both `GetHashCode()` and `Equals()` solves this problem for us.

As an additional optimization, we can ensure that the adapter doesn't generate the temporaries immediately, but instead only generates them when they are actually required. Further optimizations are possible but are domain-specific; for example, in our case lines can be parts of other lines, which would let us further save on the number of `Point` objects created.

CHAPTER 8

Bridge

One very common situation that occurs when designing software is the so-called *state space explosion,* where the number of related entities required to represent all possible states explodes in a Cartesian product fashion. For example, if you have circles and squares of different colors, you might end up with classes such as `RedSquare/BlueSquare/RedCircle/BlueCircle,` and so on. Clearly nobody wants that.

What we do instead is connect things together, and there are different ways of doing that. For example, if object color is simply a trait, we create an `enum`. If color has mutable fields, properties, or behaviors, though, we cannot restrict ourselves to an `enum`: if we do, we'll have plenty of `if/switch` statements in unrelated classes. Again, that is not something that we want.

The Bridge pattern essentially connects constituent aspects of an object using references. That's not very exciting, is it? Well, I can offer some excitement toward the end of our exploration, but we first need to take a look at a conventional implementation of the pattern.

Conventional Bridge

Let's imagine that we are interested in drawing different kinds of shapes on the screen. Suppose that we have a variety of shapes (circle, square, etc.) and also different APIs for rendering these (say, raster vs. vector rendering).

© Dmitri Nesteruk 2019
D. Nesteruk, *Design Patterns in .NET*, https://doi.org/10.1007/978-1-4842-4366-4_8

We want to create objects that specify both the type of shape and the mechanism the shape should use for rendering. How can we do this? Well, we can define an infinite bunch of classes (`RasterSquare`, `VectorCircle`, etc.) and provide an implementation for each. Alternatively, we could somehow get each shape to refer to which renderer it is using.

Let's begin by defining an `IRenderer`. This interface will determine how different shapes are rendered by whatever mechanism is required:[1]

```
public interface IRenderer
{
  void RenderCircle(float radius);
  // RenderSquare, RenderTriangle, etc.
}
```

On the other side, we can define an abstract class (not an interface) for our shape hierarchy. Why an abstract class? Because we want to keep a reference to the renderer.

```
public abstract class Shape
{
  protected IRenderer renderer;

  // a bridge between the shape that's being drawn and
  // the component that actually draws it
  public Shape(IRenderer renderer)
  {
    this.renderer = renderer;
  }
```

---

[1] I am being sly here by using a calling convention. This is done purely for illustration purposes. If every rendered shape is neither parent nor child of another shape, you can simplify this by making a series of similarly named overloads; that is, `Render(Circle c)`, `Render(Squares)`, and so on. The choice is up to you.

```
  public abstract void Draw();
  public abstract void Resize(float factor);
}
```

This might seem counterintuitive, so let's pause and ask ourselves this: What are we trying to guard against, exactly? Well, we are trying to handle two situations: when new renderers get added, and when new shapes get added to the system. We don't want either of these to spawn *multiple* changes, so here are the two situations:

- If a new shape gets added, all it has to do is inherit Shape and implement its members (say there are M different ones). Each renderer then has to implement just one new member (RenderXxx). So if there are M different renderers, the total number of operations required for a new shape is M + N.

- If a new renderer gets added, all it has to do is implement M different members, one for every shape.

As you can see, we either implement M members or M + N members. At no point do we get an M × N situation, which is what the pattern actively tries to avoid. Another added benefit is that renderers always know how to render all the shapes available in the system because each shape Xxx has a Draw() method that explicitly calls RenderXxx().

Here is the implementation of the Circle:

```
public class Circle : Shape
{
  private float radius;

  public Circle(IRenderer renderer, float radius) : base(renderer)
  {
    this.radius = radius;
  }
```

```
  public override void Draw()
  {
    renderer.RenderCircle(radius);
  }

  public override void Resize(float factor)
  {
    radius *= factor;
  }
}
```

Here is a sample implementation of one of the renderers:

```
public class VectorRenderer : IRenderer
{
  public void RenderCircle(float radius)
  {
    WriteLine($"Drawing a circle of radius {radius}");
  }
}
```

Notice that the Draw() method simply uses the bridge: It calls the corresponding renderer's drawing implementation for this particular object.

To use this setup, you have to instantiate both an IRenderer and the shape. This can be done directly:

```
var raster = new RasterRenderer();
var vector = new VectorRenderer();
var circle = new Circle(vector, 5);
circle.Draw(); // Drawing a circle of radius 5
circle.Resize(2);
circle.Draw(); // Drawing a circle of radius 10
```

If you are using a dependency injection framework, alternatively, you can define a default renderer to be used throughout the application. This way, all constructed instances of a `Circle` will be preinitialized with a renderer that is centrally defined. Here is an example that uses the Autofac container:

```
var cb = new ContainerBuilder();
cb.RegisterType<VectorRenderer>().As<IRenderer>();
cb.Register((c, p) => new Circle(c.Resolve<IRenderer>(),
  p.Positional<float>(0)));
using (var c = cb.Build())
{
  var circle = c.Resolve<Circle>(
    new PositionalParameter(0, 5.0f)
  );
  circle.Draw();
  circle.Resize(2);
  circle.Draw();
}
```

The preceding code specifies that, by default, a `VectorRenderer` should be provided when someone asks for an `IRenderer`. Furthermore, because shapes take an additional parameter (their size, presumably), we specify a default value of zero.

Dynamic Prototyping Bridge

You might have noticed that the Bridge is nothing more than the application of the dependency inversion principle, where you connect two distinct hierarchies together through a common parameter. Now we are going to take a look at a more sophisticated example involving something called Dynamic Prototyping.

Dynamic Prototyping is a technique for editing .NET programs while they are running. You have already experienced this as the Edit & Continue feature in Microsoft Visual Studio. The idea of dynamic prototyping is to allow the user to make immediate changes to the program that is currently running by editing and runtime-compiling the program's source code.

How does it work? Well, imagine you are sticking to a "one class per file" approach and you know in advance that your DI container can satisfy all dependencies of a given class. In this case you can do the following:

- Allow the user to edit the source code of this class. This works best if there is one-to-one correspondence between the class and the file. Most modern IDEs try to enforce this approach.

- After you edit and save the new source code, use the C# compiler to compile just that class and get an in-memory implementation of the new type. You basically get a System.Type. You could, if you wanted, just instantiate that new type and use it to update some reference.

- Change the registration options in the DI container so that your new type is now a replacement for the original type. This naturally requires that you are using abstractions of some kind.

The last point needs explaining. If you have a concrete type Foo.Bar and you build a brand new, in-memory type Foo.Bar then, even if the APIs of those types stay the same, those types are *incompatible*. You cannot assign a reference to the old Bar with the new one. The only way to use them interchangeably is via dynamic or reflection, and both of those are niche cases.

Let me illustrate how the entire process works. Suppose you have a Log class being used by a Payroll class. Using hypothetical dependency injection, you could define it as:

```
// Log.cs
public class Log
{
  void Info(string msg) { ... }
}

// Payroll.cs
public class Payroll
{
  [Service]
  public Log Log { get; set; }
}
```

Notice that I'm defining the Log as an injected property, not via constructor injection. Now, to make a dynamic bridge, you would introduce an interface; that is:

```
// ILog.cs
public interface ILog
{
  void Info(string msg);
}

// Log.cs
public class Log : ILog { /* as before */ }
```

```
// Payroll.cs
public class Payroll
{
  [Service]
  public ILog Log { get; set; }
}
```

Pay attention to the names of files, too. This is important, as each type is in its own file. Now, as you run this program, suppose you want to change the implementation of Log without stopping the application. You would do this:

- Open an editor with the Log.cs file and edit the file.

- Close the editor. Now Log.cs gets compiled into an in-memory assembly.

- Create the first type found in this new assembly. It will be a Log, for sure, but incompatible with the previous Log! However, it implements an ILog, which is good enough for us.

- Go over the objects already created by the container and update all [Service]-marked references to an ILog with the new object.

This last part could be tricky. First, you need a container that can go over its own injection points. To be honest, though, you could use good old-fashioned reflection for this purpose, too. The reason I am referring to a container is that it is more convenient to use. Also, notice this approach only works for property injection, and there is an implicit assumption that the service is *immutable* (has no state). If the service had state, you'd have to serialize it and then deserialize the data into the new object—not impossible, but a robust implementation needs to handle many corner cases.

The moral of this story is that, to be able to substitute one runtime-constructed type for another, they both need to implement the same interface. Before you ask, you cannot dynamically change any base type (class or interface).

Summary

The principal goal of the Bridge design pattern, as we have seen, is to avoid excessive proliferation of data types where there are two or more dimensions, or aspects of a system that can potentially multiply in number. The best approach to Bridge is still active avoidance (e.g., replace classes with enums, if possible), but if that is not possible, simply abstract away both hierarchies and find a way of connecting them.

CHAPTER 9

Composite

It's a fact of life that objects are quite often composed of other objects (or, in other words, they aggregate other objects). Remember, we agreed to equate aggregation and composition at the start of this part of the book.

There are a few ways for an object to advertise that it is composed of something. The most obvious approach is for an object to either implement IEnumerable<T> (where T is whatever you're prepared to expose) or, alternatively, to expose public members that themselves implement IEnumerable<T>.

Another option for advertising being a composite is to inherit from a known collection class such as Collection<T>, List<T>, or something similar. This of course lets you not just implement IEnumerable<T> implicitly, but also provides you with an internal storage mechanism, so issues such as adding new objects to the collection are automatically handled for you.

So what is the Composite pattern about? Essentially, we try to give single objects and groups of objects an identical interface and have those interface members work correctly regardless of which class is the underlying one.

Grouping Graphic Objects

Think of an application such as Microsoft PowerPoint where you can select several different objects and drag them as one. Yet, if you were to select a single object, you could grab that object, too. The same goes for rendering:

© Dmitri Nesteruk 2019
D. Nesteruk, *Design Patterns in .NET*, https://doi.org/10.1007/978-1-4842-4366-4_9

you can render an individual graphic object, or you can group several shapes together and they get drawn as one group.

The implementation of this approach is rather easy because it relies on just a single base class such as the following:

```
public class GraphicObject
{
  public virtual string Name { get; set; } = "Group";
  public string Color;
  // todo members
}
public class Circle : GraphicObject
{
  public override string Name => "Circle";
}
public class Square : GraphicObject
{
  public override string Name => "Square";
}
```

This appears to be a fairly ordinary example with nothing standing out except for the fact that GraphicObject is abstract, as well as the virtual string Name property, which is, for some reason, set to "Group". Even though the inheritors of GraphicObject are, obviously, scalar entities, GraphicObject itself reserves the right to act as a *container* for further items.

This is done by furnishing GraphicObject with a lazily constructed list of children:

```
public class GraphicObject
{
  ...
  private Lazy<List<GraphicObject>> children =
    new Lazy<List<GraphicObject>>();
```

```
  public List<GraphicObject> Children => children.Value;
}
```

GraphicObject can therefore act as both a singular, scalar element
(e.g., you inherit it and you get a Circle), but it can also be used as a
container of elements. We can implement some methods that would print
its contents:

```
public class GraphicObject
{
  private void Print(StringBuilder sb, int depth)
  {
    sb.Append(new string('*', depth))
      .Append(string.IsNullOrWhiteSpace(Color) ? string.Empty :
      $"{Color} ")
      .AppendLine($"{Name}");
    foreach (var child in Children)
      child.Print(sb, depth + 1);
  }

  public override string ToString()
  {
    var sb = new StringBuilder();
    Print(sb, 0);
    return sb.ToString();
  }
}
```

The preceding code uses asterisks to indicate the level of depth of each
element. Armed with this, we can now construct a drawing that consists of
both shapes and groups of shapes and print it out:

```
var drawing = new GraphicObject {Name = "My Drawing"};
drawing.Children.Add(new Square {Color = "Red"});
drawing.Children.Add(new Circle{Color="Yellow"});
```

133

```
var group = new GraphicObject();
group.Children.Add(new Circle{Color="Blue"});
group.Children.Add(new Square{Color="Blue"});
drawing.Children.Add(group);

WriteLine(drawing);
```

Here is the output we get:

```
My Drawing
*Red Square
*Yellow Circle
*Group
**Blue Circle
**Blue Square
```

This is the simplest implementation of the Composite design pattern that is based on inheritance and optional containment of a list of subelements. The only issue, which the astute reader will recognize, is that it makes absolutely no sense for scalar classes such as `Circle` or `Square` to have a `Children` member. What if someone were to use such an API? It would make very little sense.

In the next example we look at scalar objects that are truly scalar, with no extraneous members in their interface.

Neural Networks

Machine learning is the hot new thing, and part of machine learning is the use of artificial neural networks, software constructs that attempt to mimic the way neurons work in our brains.

The central concept of neural networks is, of course, a *neuron*. A neuron can produce a (typically numeric) output as a function of its inputs, and we can feed that value on to other connections in the network. We are going to concern ourselves with connections only, so we'll model the neuron like so:

```
public class Neuron
{
  public List<Neuron> In, Out;
}
```

This is a simple neuron with outgoing and incoming connections to other neurons. You probably want to be able to connect one neuron to another, which can be done using

```
public void ConnectTo(Neuron other)
{
  Out.Add(other);
  other.In.Add(this);
}
```

This method does fairly predictable things: It sets up connections between the current (this) neuron and some other one. So far so good. Now, suppose we also want to create neuron *layers*. A layer is quite simply a specific number of neurons grouped together. This can easily be done just by inheriting from a Collection<T>; that is:

```
public class NeuronLayer : Collection<Neuron>
{
  public NeuronLayer(int count)
  {
    while (count --> 0)
      Add(new Neuron());
  }
}
```

That looks good, right? I've even thrown in the operator --> for you to enjoy.[1] Now, though, we have a bit of a problem. The problem is this: we want to be able to have neurons connectable to neuron layers. Broadly speaking, we want this to work:

```
var neuron1 = new Neuron();
var neuron2 = new Neuron();
var layer1 = new NeuronLayer(3);
var layer2 = new NeuronLayer(4);

neuron1.ConnectTo(neuron2); // works already :)
neuron1.ConnectTo(layer1);
layer2.ConnectTo(neuron1);
layer1.ConnectTo(layer2);
```

As you can see, we have four distinct cases to take care of:

1. Neuron connecting to another neuron.

2. Neuron connecting to layer.

3. Layer connecting to neuron.

4. Layer connecting to another layer.

As you might have guessed, there's no way in Baator that we'll be making four overloads of the ConnectTo() method. What if there were three distinct classes? Would we realistically consider creating nine methods? I do not think so.

The way to have a single-method solution to this problem is to realize that both Neuron and NeuronLayer can be treated as enumerables. In the case of a NeuronLayer, there's no problem, but in the case of Neuron, we need to do some work.

---

[1]There is, of course, no --> operator; it's quite simply the postfix decrement -- followed by greater than >. The effect, though, is exactly as the --> arrow suggests: in while (count --> 0) we iterate until count reaches zero.

To get Neuron ready, we are going to do the following:

- Remove its own ConnectTo() method, as it is not general enough.

- Implement the IEnumerable<Neuron> interface, yielding ourself (!) when someone wants to enumerate us.

Here's what the new Neuron class looks like:

```
public class Neuron : IEnumerable<Neuron>
{
  public List<Neuron> In, Out;

  public IEnumerator<Neuron> GetEnumerator()
  {
    yield return this;
  }

  IEnumerator IEnumerable.GetEnumerator()
  {
    return GetEnumerator();
  }
}
```

Now, the *piece de resistance*: Because both Neuron and NeuronLayer now conform to IEnumerable<Neuron>, all that remains for us to do is implement a single extension method that connects the two enumerables together:

```
public static class ExtensionMethods
{
  public static void ConnectTo(
    this IEnumerable<Neuron> self, IEnumerable<Neuron> other)
  {
    if (ReferenceEquals(self, other)) return;
```

```
  foreach (var from in self)
    foreach (var to in other)
    {
      from.Out.Add(to);
      to.In.Add(from);
    }
  }
}
```

That's it! We now have a single method that can be called to glue together any entities consisting of Neuron classes. Now, if we decided to make some NeuronRing, provided it supports IEnumerable<Neuron>, we can easily connect it to either a Neuron, a NeuronLayer, or another NeuronRing!

Shrink Wrapping the Composite

No doubt many of you want some kind of prepackaged solution that would allow scalar objects to be treated as enumerables. Well, if your scalar class doesn't derive from another class, you can simply define a base class similar to the following:

```
public abstract class Scalar<T> : IEnumerable<T>
  where T : Scalar<T>
{
  public IEnumerator<T> GetEnumerator()
  {
    yield return (T) this;
  }
```

```
IEnumerator IEnumerable.GetEnumerator()
{
  return GetEnumerator();
}
}
```

This class is generic, and the type parameter T refers to the object we are trying to "scalarize." Now, making any object expose itself as a collection of one element is as simple as this:

```
public class Foo : Scalar<Foo> {}
```

and the object is immediately available for use in, say, a foreach loop:

```
var foo = new Foo();
foreach (var x in foo)
{
  // will yield only one value of x
  // where x == foo referentially :)
}
```

This approach only works if your type doesn't have a parent because multiple inheritance is impossible. It would, of course, be nice to have some marker interface (inheriting from IEnumerable<T>, perhaps, although that's not strictly necessary) that would implement GetEnumerator() as extension methods. Sadly, the C# language designers did not leave this option available—GetEnumerator() must strictly be *instance* methods to be picked up by foreach.

Summary

The Composite design pattern allows us to provide identical interfaces for individual objects and collections of objects. This can be accomplished in one of two ways:

- Make every scalar object you intend to work with a collection or, alternatively, get it to contain a collection and expose it somehow. You can use `Lazy<T>` so you don't allocate too many data structures if they are not actually needed. This is a very simple approach and is somewhat unidiomatic.

- Teach scalar objects to appear as collections. This is done by implementing `IEnumerable<T>` and then calling `yield return this` in `GetEnumerator()`. Strictly speaking, having a scalar value expose `IEnumerable` is also unidiomatic, but it is aesthetically better and has a smaller computational cost.

CHAPTER 10

Decorator

Suppose you're working with a class your colleague wrote, and you want to extend that class's functionality. How would you do it without modifying the original code? One approach is inheritance: You make a derived class, add the functionality you need, maybe even override something, and you're good to go.

Right, except this doesn't always work, and there are many reasons why. The most common reason is that you cannot inherit the class, either because your target class needs to inherit something else (and multiple inheritance is impossible) or because the class you want to extend is sealed.

The Decorator pattern allows us to enhance existing types without either modifying the original types (Open-Closed Principle) or causing an explosion of the number of derived types.

Custom String Builder

Suppose you are into code generation and you want to extend StringBuilder to offer additional utility methods such as supporting indentation or scopes or whatever code generation functionality makes sense. It would be nice to simply inherit from StringBuilder, but it is sealed (for security reasons). Also, because you might want to store the current indentation level (say, to provide Indent()/Unindent() methods),

© Dmitri Nesteruk 2019
D. Nesteruk, *Design Patterns in .NET*, https://doi.org/10.1007/978-1-4842-4366-4_10

you cannot simply go ahead and use extension methods, as those are stateless.[1]

The solution is to create a Decorator, a brand new class that aggregates a StringBuilder but also stores and exposes the same members as StringBuilder did, and a few more. From the outset, the class can look as follows:

```
public class CodeBuilder
{
  private StringBuilder builder = new StringBuilder();
  private int indentLevel = 0;

  public CodeBuilder Indent()
  {
    indentLevel++;
    return this;
  }
}
```

As you can see, we have both the underlying StringBuilder as well as some additional members related to the extended functionality. What we need to do now is expose the members of StringBuilder as members of CodeBuilder, delegating the calls. StringBuilder has a very large API, so doing this by hand is unreasonable: instead, what you would do is use code generation (e.g., ReSharper's **Generate | Delegated members**) to automatically create the necessary API.

---

[1]Strictly speaking, it *is* possible to store state in extension methods, albeit in a very roundabout way. Essentially, what you would do is have your extension class keep a static member of type Dictionary<WeakReference, Dictionary<string,object>> and then modify the entries in this dictionary to map an object to its set of properties. Plenty of fiddling is required here, both in terms of working with weak references (we don't want this store to extend the lifetime of the original object, right?) as well as the boxing and unboxing that comes with storing a bunch of objects.

This operation can be applied to every single member of StringBuilder and will generate the following signatures:

```
public class CodeBuilder
{
  public StringBuilder Append(string value)
  {
    return builder.Append(value);
  }

  public StringBuilder AppendLine()
  {
    return builder.AppendLine();
  }
  // other generated members omitted
}
```

This might seem great at first glance, but the implementation is actually incorrect. Remember, StringBuilder exposes a fluent API to be able to write things like

```
myBuilder.Append("Hello").AppendLine(" World");
```

In other words, it provides a fluent interface, but our Decorator does not! For example, it won't let us write myBuilder.Append("x"). Indent() because the result of Append(), as generated by ReSharper, is a StringBuilder that doesn't have an Indent() member. That's right: ReSharper does not know that we want a proper fluent interface. What you want is the fluent calls in CodeBuilder to appear as:

```
public class CodeBuilder
{
  public CodeBuilder Append(char value, int repeatCount)
  {
    builder.Append(value, repeatCount);
```

```
    return this; // return a CodeBuilder, not a StringBuilder
  }
  ...
}
```

This is something that you would need to fix by hand or possibly through regular expressions. This modification, when applied to every single call that is delegated to `StringBuilder`, would allow us to chain `StringBuilder`'s calls together with our unique, `CodeBuilder`-specific ones.

Adapter-Decorator

You can also have a Decorator that acts as an adapter. For example, suppose we want to take the `CodeBuilder` from the preceding example, but we want it to start acting like a `string`. Perhaps we want to take a `CodeBuilder` and stick it into an API that expects our object to implement the = operator for assigning from a `string` and a += operator for appending additional strings. Can we adapt `CodeBuilder` to these requirements? We sure can; all we have to do is add the appropriate functionality:

```
public static implicit operator CodeBuilder(string s)
{
  var cb = new CodeBuilder();
  cb.sb.Append(s);
  return cb;
}

public static CodeBuilder operator +(CodeBuilder cb, string s)
{
  cb.Append(s);
  return cb;
}
```

Now we can write something like the following:

```
CodeBuilder cb = "hello ";
cb += "world";
WriteLine(cb);
```

Curiously enough, the second line in this will work even if we didn't implement the operator + explicitly. Why? You figure it out!

Multiple Inheritance

In addition to extending sealed classes, the Decorator also shows up when you want to have multiple base classes, which of course you cannot have because C# does not support multiple inheritance. For example, suppose you have a dragon that is both a bird and a lizard. It would make sense to write something like this:

```
public class Bird
{
  public void Fly() { ... }
}

public class Lizard
{
  public void Crawl() { ... }
}

public class Dragon : Bird, Lizard {} // cannot do this!
```

Sadly, this is impossible, so what do you do? Well, you extract interfaces from both Bird and Lizard:

```
public interface IBird
{
  void Fly();
}
```

145

```
public interface ILizard
{
  void Crawl();
}
```

Then you make a Dragon class that implements these interfaces, aggregates instances of Bird and Lizard, and delegates the calls:

```
public class Dragon: IBird, ILizard
{
  private readonly IBird bird;
  private readonly ILizard lizard;

  public Dragon(IBird bird, ILizard lizard)
  {
    this.bird = bird;
    this.lizard = lizard;
  }

  public void Crawl()
  {
    lizard.Crawl();
  }

  public void Fly()
  {
    bird.Fly();
  }
}
```

You'll notice that there are two options here: either you initialize the default instances of Bird and Lizard right inside the class or you offer the client more flexibility by taking both of those objects in the constructor. This would allow you to construct more sophisticated IBird/ILizard classes and make a dragon out of them. Also, this approach automatically supports constructor injection, should you go the IoC route.

One interesting problem with the Decorator is the 'diamond inheritance' problem of C++. Suppose a dragon crawls only until it is 10 years old and, from then on, it only flies. In this case, you'd have both the Bird and Lizard classes have an Age property with independent implementations:

```
public interface ICreature
{
  int Age { get; set; }
}

public interface IBird : ICreature
{
  void Fly();
}

public interface ILizard : ICreature
{
  void Crawl();
}

public class Bird : IBird
{
  public int Age { get; set; }
  public void Fly()
  {
    if (Age >= 10)
      WriteLine("I am flying!");
  }
}
```

```
public class Lizard : ILizard
{
  public int Age { get; set; }
  public void Crawl()
  {
    if (Age < 10)
      WriteLine("I am crawling!");
  }
}
```

Notice that we've had to introduce a new interface ICreature just so we could expose the Age as part of both the IBird and ILizard interfaces. The real problem here is the implementation of the Dragon class, because if you use the code generation features of ReSharer or a similar tool, you will simply get this:

```
public class Dragon : IBird, ILizard
{
  ...
  public int Age { get; set; }
}
```

This once again shows that generated code is not always what you want. Remember, both Bird.Fly() and Lizard.Crawl() have their own implementations of Age, and those implementations need to be kept consistent for those methods to operate correctly. This means that the correct implementation of Dragon.Age is the following:

```
public int Age
{
  get => bird.Age;
  set => bird.Age = lizard.Age = value;
}
```

Notice that our setter assigns both, whereas the getter simply uses the underlying bird—this choice is arbitrary, and we could have easily taken the lizard's age instead. The setter ensures consistency, so in theory, both values would always be equal, except during initialization, a place we haven't taken care of yet. A lazy man's solution to this problem would be to redefine the Dragon constructor thus:

```
public Dragon(IBird bird, ILizard lizard)
{
  this.bird = bird;
  this.lizard = lizard;
  bird.Age = lizard.Age;
}
```

As you can see, building a Decorator is generally easy, except for two nuances: the difficulties in preserving a fluent interface, and the challenge of diamond inheritance. I have demonstrated here how to solve both of these problems.

Dynamic Decorator Composition

Of course, as soon as we start building Decorators over existing types, we come to the question of decorator *composition*; that is, whether or not it is possible to decorate a Decorator with another Decorator (in other words, to apply two or more decorators to an object). I certainly hope it is possible; Decorators should be flexible enough to do this!

For our scenario, let's imagine that we have an abstract base class called Shape with a single member called AsString() that returns a string describing this shape (I am deliberately avoiding ToString() here):

```
public abstract class Shape
{
  public virtual string AsString() => string.Empty;
}
```

I chose to make Shape an abstract class with a default, no-op implementation. We could equally use an IShape interface for this example.

We can now define a concrete shape like, say, a circle or a square:

```
public sealed class Circle : Shape
{
  private float radius;

  public Circle() : this(0)
  {

  }

  public Circle(float radius)
  {
    this.radius = radius;
  }

  public void Resize(float factor)
  {
    radius *= factor;
  }

  public override string AsString() => $"A circle of radius
  {radius}";
}

// similar implementation of Square with 'side' member omitted
```

I deliberately made Circle and similar classes sealed so we cannot go ahead and simply inherit from them. Instead, we are once again going to build Decorators: this time, we will build two of them. The first one is for adding color to a shape:

```csharp
public class ColoredShape : Shape
{
  private readonly Shape shape;
  private readonly string color;

  public ColoredShape(Shape shape, string color)
  {
    this.shape = shape;
    this.color = color;
  }

  public override string AsString()
    => $"{shape.AsString()} has the color {color}";
}
```

and another to give a shape transparency:

```csharp
public class TransparentShape : Shape
{
  private readonly Shape shape;
  private readonly float transparency;

  public TransparentShape(Shape shape, float transparency)
  {
    this.shape = shape;
    this.transparency = transparency;
  }

  public override string AsString() =>
    $"{shape.AsString()} has {transparency * 100.0f}%
    transparency";
}
```

As you can see, both of these Decorators inherit from the abstract Shape class, so they are themselves Shapes and they decorate other Shapes by taking them in the constructor. This allows us to use them together; for example:

```
var circle = new Circle(2);
WriteLine(circle.AsString());
// A circle of radius 2

var redSquare = new ColoredShape(circle, "red");
WriteLine(redSquare.AsString());
// A circle of radius 2 has the color red

var redHalfTransparentSquare = new TransparentShape(redSquare,
0.5f);
WriteLine(redHalfTransparentSquare.AsString());
// A circle of radius 2 has the color red has 50% transparency
```

As you can see, the Decorators can be applied to other Shapes in any order you wish, preserving consistent output of the AsString() method. One thing they do not guard against is cyclic repetition: you can construct a ColoredShape(ColoredShape(Square)) and the system will not complain; we could not detect this situation either, even if we wanted to.

This is the *dynamic* Decorator implementation: We call it dynamic because these Decorators can be constructed at runtime, objects wrapping objects as layers of an onion. It is very convenient, but you lose all type information as you decorate the object. For example, a decorated Circle no longer has access to its Resize() member:

```
var redSquare = new ColoredShape(circle, "red");
redCircle.Resize(2); // oops!
```

This problem is impossible to solve: because ColoredShape takes a Shape, the only way to allow resizing is to add Resize() to Shape itself, but this operation might not make sense for all shapes. This is a limitation of the dynamic Decorator.

Static Decorator

When you are given a dynamically decorated ColorShape, there is no way to tell whether this shape is a circle, square, or something else without looking at the output of AsString(). How would you "bake in" the underlying type of the decorated objects to the type of the object you have? As it turns out, you can do so with generics.

The idea is simple: our Decorator, say, ColoredShape, takes a generic argument that specifies what type of object it is decorating. Naturally, that object has to be a Shape, and because we are aggregating it, it is also going to need a constructor:

```
public class ColoredShape<T> : Shape
  where T : Shape, new()
{
  private readonly string color;
  private readonly T shape = new T();

  public ColoredShape() : this("black") {}
  public ColoredShape(string color) { this.color = color; }

  public override string AsString() =>
    return $"{shape.AsString()} has the color {color}";
}
```

Okay, so what's going on here? We have a new ColoredShape that is generic, and it takes a T that is supposed to inherit a Shape. Internally, it stores an instance of T as well as color information. We have provided two constructors for flexibility: because C#, unlike C++, doesn't support constructor forwarding, the default constructor is going to be useful for composition (see, we have the new() requirement).

We can now provide a similar implementation of TransparentShape<T> and, armed with both, we can now build static Decorators of the following form:

```
ColoredShape<Circle> blueCircle = new
ColoredShape<Circle>("blue");
WriteLine(blueCircle.AsString());
// A circle of radius 0 has the color blue

TransparentShape<ColoredShape<Square>> blackHalfSquare = new
TransparentShape<ColoredShape<Square>>(0.4f);
WriteLine(blackHalfSquare.AsString());
// A square with side 0 has the color black has transparency 40
```

This static approach has certain advantages and disadvantages. The advantage is that we preserve the type information: given a Shape we can tell that the shape is a ColoredShape<Circle> and perhaps we can act on this information somehow. Sadly, this approach has plenty of disadvantages:

- Notice how the radius and side values in the example given are both zero. This is because we cannot initialize those values in the constructor: C# does not have constructor forwarding.

- We still don't have access to the underlying members; for example, blueCircle.Resize() is still not legal.

- These sorts of Decorators cannot be composed at runtime.

All in all, in the absence of (CRTP) Curiously Recurring Template Pattern[2] and mixin inheritance[3], the uses for static Decorators in C# are very, very limited.

Functional Decorator

A functional Decorator is a natural consequence of functional composition. If we can compose functions, we can equally wrap functions with other functions, for example, to provide before-and-after functionality such as logging.

Here is a very simple implementation. Imagine you have some work that needs to be done:

```
let doWork() =
  printfn "Doing some work"
```

We can now create a decorator function (a functional Decorator) that, given any function, measures how long it takes to execute:

```
let logger work name =
  let sw = Stopwatch.StartNew()
  printfn "%s %s" "Entering method" name
  work()
  sw.Stop()
  printfn "Exiting method %s; %fs elapsed" name sw.Elapsed.
  TotalSeconds
```

---

[2]CRTP is a popular C++ pattern that looks like this: class Foo<T> : T. In other words, you inherit from a generic parameter, something that is impossible in C#.

[3]Mixin inheritance is a C++ technique for adding functionality to classes by using inheritance. In the context of the Decorator, it would allow us to compose a class of type T<U<V>> that would inherit from both U and V, giving us access to all the underlying members. Also, constructors would work correctly thanks to constructor forwarding and C++'s variadic templates.

We can now use this wrapper around doWork, replacing a unit -> unit function with one with the same interface but that also performs some measurements:

```
let loggedWork() = logger doWork "doWork"
loggedWork()
// Entering method doWork
// Doing some work
// Exiting method doWork; 0.097824 s elapsed
```

Pay attention to the round brackets in this example: It might be tempting to remove them, but that would drastically alter the types of data structures. Remember, any let x = ... construct will always evaluate to a variable (possibly of a unit type) instead of a parameterless function unless you add an empty argument list.

There are a couple of catches in this implementation. For one, doWork does not return a value; if it did, we would have to cache it in a type-independent manner, something that is possible to implement in C++ but extremely difficult to do in any .NET language. Another issue is that we have no way of determining the name of the wrapped function, so we end up passing it as a separate argument, which is not an ideal solution!

Summary

A Decorator gives a class additional functionality while adhering to the OCP and mitigating issues related to sealed classes and multiple inheritance. Its crucial aspect is *composability*: Several Decorators can be applied to an object in any order. We've looked at the following types of Decorators:

- Dynamic Decorators, which can store references to the decorated objects and provide dynamic (runtime) composability.

- Static Decorators, which preserve the information about the type of the objects involved in the decoration; these are of limited use because they do not expose underlying objects' members, nor do they allow us to efficiently compose constructor calls.

In both of the cases, we completely ignored the issues related to cyclic use: nothing in the API prevents applying the same static or dynamic Decorator more than once.

CHAPTER 11

Façade

First of all, let's get the linguistic issue out of the way: That little curve in the letter ç is called a *cedilla* and the letter itself is pronounced as an S, so the word façade is pronounced *fah-saad*. The particularly pedantic among you are welcome to use the letter ç in your code, as compilers handle this just fine.[1]

Now, let's learn about the pattern itself. Essentially, the best analogy I can think of is a typical house. When you buy a house, you generally care about the exterior and the interior. You are less concerned about the internals: electrical systems, insulation, sanitation, that sort of thing. Those parts are all equally important, but we want them to "just work" without breaking. You are much more likely to be buying new furniture than changing the wiring of your boiler.

The same idea applies to software: Sometimes you need to interact with a complicated system in a simple way. By *system* we could mean a set of components or just a single component with a rather complicated API. For example, think about the seemingly simple task of downloading a string of text from a URL. The fully fleshed-out solution to this problem using various System.Net data types looks like something like the following:

---

[1]Over the years I have seen many tricks involving the use of Unicode (typically UTF-8) encoding in C# source files. The most insidious case is one where a developer insisted on calling his extension method's first argument this—it was, of course, a completely valid identifier because the letter i in this was a Ukrainian letter і, not a Latin one.

```
string url = "http://www.google.com/robots.txt";
var request = WebRequest.Create(url);
request.Credentials = CredentialCache.DefaultCredentials;
var response = request.GetResponse();
var dataStream = response.GetResponseStream();
var reader = new StreamReader(dataStream);
string responseFromServer = reader.ReadToEnd();
Console.WriteLine(responseFromServer);
reader.Close();
response.Close();
```

This is a lot of work! Furthermore, I almost guarantee that most of you would not be able to write this code without looking it up on Microsoft Developer Network (MSDN). That's because there are several underlying data types that make the operation possible. If you wanted to do it all asynchronously, you would have to use a complementary API set comprised of XxxAsync() methods.

So whenever we encounter a situation where a complex interaction of different parts is required for something to get done, we might want to put it behind a façade; that is, a much simpler interface. In the case of downloading web pages, all of this reduces to a single line:

```
new WebClient().DownloadString(url);
```

In this example, the WebClient class is the façade; that is, a nice, user-friendly interface that does what you want quickly and without ceremony. Of course, the original APIs are also available to you so that, if you need something more complicated (e.g., to provide credentials), you can use the more technical parts to fine-tune the operation of your program.

With this one example, you've already grasped the gist of the Façade design pattern. However, to illustrate the matter further (as well as tell the story of how OOP is used and abused in practice), I would like to present yet another example.

Building a Trading Terminal

I have spent a lot of time working in areas of quant finance and algorithmic trading. As you can probably guess, what's required of a good trading terminal is quick delivery of information into a trader's brain: you want things to be rendered as fast as possible, without any lag.

Most financial data (except for charts) is actually rendered in plain text: white characters on a black screen. This is, in a way, similar to the way the terminal, console, and command-line interface works in your own operating system, but there is a subtle difference. The first part of a terminal window is the *buffer*. This is where the rendered characters are stored. A buffer is a rectangular area of memory, typically a $1D^2$ or 2D char or wchar_t array. A buffer can be much larger than the visible area of the terminal window, so it can store some historical output to which you can scroll back.

Typically, a buffer has a pointer (e.g., an integer) specifying the current input line. That way, a full buffer doesn't reallocate all lines; it just overwrites the oldest one.

Then there is the idea of a *viewport*. A viewport renders a part of the particular buffer. A buffer can be huge, so a viewport just takes a rectangular area out of that buffer and renders that (see Figure 11-1). Naturally, the size of the viewport has to be less than or equal to the size of the buffer.

---

[2]Most buffers are typically one-dimensional because it is easier to pass a single pointer somewhere than a double pointer, and using an array or vector does not make much sense when the size of the structure is deterministic and immutable. Another advantage to the 1D approach is that, when it comes to GPU processing, a system such as CUDA uses up to six dimensions for addressing anyway, so after a while, computing a 1D index from an N-dimensional block/grid position becomes second nature.

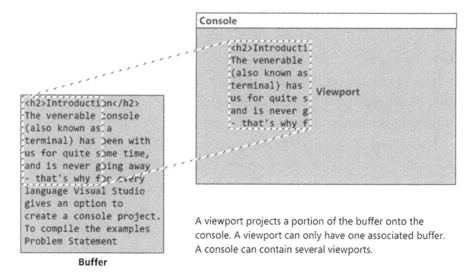

Figure 11-1. *Illustration of a buffer and a viewport*

Finally, there's the console (terminal window) itself. The console shows the viewport, allows scrolling up and down, and even accepts user input. The console is, in fact, a façade: a simplified representation of what is a rather complicated setup behind the scenes.

Typically, most users interact with a single buffer and viewport. It is possible, however, to have a console window where you have, say, the area split vertically between two viewports, each having its corresponding buffers. This can be done using utilities such as the `screen` Linux command.

An Advanced Terminal

One problem with a typical operating system terminal is that it is *extremely slow* if you pipe a lot of data into it. For example, a Windows terminal window (`cmd.exe`) uses Graphic Device Interface (GDI) to render the characters, which is completely unnecessary. In a fast-paced trading environment, you want the rendering to be hardware-accelerated:

Characters should be presented as prerendered textures placed on a surface using an API such as OpenGL.[3]

A trading terminal consists of multiple buffers and viewports. In a typical setup, different buffers might be getting updated concurrently with data from various exchanges or trading bots, and all of this information needs to be presented on a single screen.

Buffers also provide functionality that is a lot more exciting than just 1D or 2D linear storage. For example, a TableBuffer might be defined as:

```
public class TableBuffer : IBuffer
{
  private readonly TableColumnSpec[] spec;
  private readonly int totalHeight;
  private readonly List<string[]> buffer;
  private static readonly Point invalidPoint = new Point(-1,-1);
  private readonly short[,] formatBuffer;

  public TableBuffer(TableColumnSpec [] spec, int totalHeight)
  {
    this.spec = spec;
    this.totalHeight = totalHeight;

    buffer = new List<string[]>();
    for (int i = 0; i < (totalHeight - 1); ++i)
    {
      buffer.Add(new string[spec.Length]);
    }

    formatBuffer = new short[spec.Max(s => s.Width),totalHeight];
  }
```

---

[3]We also use ASCII, because Unicode is rarely, if ever, required. Having 1 char = 1 byte is a good practice if you don't need to support extra character sets. Although not relevant to the discussion at hand, it also greatly simplifies the implementation of string processing algorithms on both Graphics Processing Units (GPUs) and Field-Programmable Gate Arrays (FPGAs).

```
public struct TableColumnSpec
{
  public string Header;
  public int Width;
  public TableColumnAlignment Alignment;
}
}
```

In other words, a buffer can take some specification and build a table (yes, a good, old-fashioned, ASCII-formatted table) and present it on screen.[4]

A viewport is in charge of getting data from the buffer. Some of its characteristics include the following:

- A reference to the buffer it is showing.

- Its size.

- If the viewport is smaller than the buffer, it needs to specify which part of the buffer it is going to show. This is expressed in absolute x, y coordinates.

- The location of the viewport on the overall console window.

- The location of the cursor, assuming this viewport is currently taking user input.

---

[4]Many trading terminals have abandoned pure ASCII representation in favor of more mixed-mode approaches, such as simply using monospace fonts in ordinary UI controls or rendering many little text-based consoles in a separate windowing API rather than sticking to a single canvas.

Where's the Façade?

The console itself is the façade in this particular system. Internally, the console has to manage a lot of different internal settings:

```
public class Console : Form
{
  private readonly Device device;
  private readonly PresentParameters pp;
  private IList<Viewport> viewports;
  private Size charSize;
  private Size gridSize;
  // many more fields here
}
```

Initialization of the console is also, typically, a very nasty affair. At the very least, you need to specify the size of individual characters and the width and height of the console (in terms of the number of characters). In some situations, you do actually want to specify console parameters in excruciating detail but, when in a hurry, you just want a sensible set of defaults.

However, because it is a Façade, it actually tries to give a really accessible API. This might take a number of sensible parameters from which to initialize all the guts.

```
private Console(bool fullScreen, int charWidth, int charHeight,
  int width, int height, Size? clientSize)
{
  int windowWidth =
    clientSize == null ? charWidth*width : clientSize.Value.
    Width;
  int windowHeight =
    clientSize == null ? charHeight*height : clientSize.Value.
    Height;
```

```
// and a lot more code

// single buffer and viewport created here
// linked together and added to appropriate collections
// image textures generated
// grid size calculated depending on whether we want
   fullscreen mode
}
```

Alternatively, one might pack all those arguments into a single object that, again, has some sensible defaults:

```
public static Console Create(ConsoleCreationParameters ccp)
{ ... }

public class ConsoleCreationParameters
{
  public Size? ClientSize;
  public int CharacterWidth = 10;
  public int CharacterHeight = 14;
  public int Width = 20;
  public int Height = 30;
  public bool FullScreen;
  public bool CreateDefaultViewAndBuffer = true;
}
```

As you can see, with the Façade we've built, there are no fewer than three ways of setting up the console:

- Use the low-level API to configure the console explicitly, viewports and buffers included.

- Use the Console constructor, which requires you to provide fewer values, and makes a couple of useful assumptions (e.g., that you want just one viewport with an underlying buffer).

- Use the constructor that takes a
  `ConsoleCreationParameters` object. This requires you
  to provide even fewer pieces of information, as every
  field of that structure has a suitable default. Setting
  sensible defaults is a good practice in all areas of
  programming.

Summary

The Façade design pattern is a way of putting a simple interface in front of
one or more complicated subsystems. In our example, a complicated setup
involving many buffers and viewports can be used directly or, if you just
want a simple console with a single buffer and associated viewport, you
can get it through a very accessible and intuitive API.

CHAPTER 12

Flyweight

A Flyweight (also sometimes called a *token* or a *cookie*) is a temporary component that acts as a smart reference to something. Typically, Flyweights are used in situations where you have a very large number of very similar objects, and you want to minimize the amount of memory that is dedicated to storing all these values. Let's take a look at some scenarios where this pattern becomes relevant.

Usernames

Imagine a massively multiplayer online game. I bet you $20 there will be more than one user called John Smith, quite simply because it is a popular name. If we were to store that name over and over (in UTF-16), we would be spending ten characters (plus a few more bytes for every `string`). Instead, we could store the name once and then store a reference to every user with that name. That's quite a saving.

Furthermore, the last name Smith is likely very popular on its own. Thus, instead of storing full names, splitting the name into first and last would allow further optimizations, as you could store `"Smith"` in an indexed store and then simply store the index value instead of the actual string.

Let's see how we can implement such a space-saving system. We are actually going to do this scientifically by forcing garbage collection (GC) and measuring the amount of memory taken using dotMemory.

© Dmitri Nesteruk 2019
D. Nesteruk, *Design Patterns in .NET*, https://doi.org/10.1007/978-1-4842-4366-4_12

Here's the first, naive implementation of a User class. Notice that the full name is kept as a single string.

```
public class User
{
  public string FullName { get; }

  public User(string fullName)
  {
    FullName = fullName;
  }
}
```

The implication of this code is that "John Smith" and "Jane Smith" are distinct strings, each occupying its own memory. Now we can construct an alternative type, User2, that is a little bit smarter in terms of its storage while exposing the same API (I've avoided extracting an IUser interface here for brevity):

```
public class User2
{
  private static List<string> strings = new List<string>();
  private int[] names;

  public User2(string fullName)
  {
    int getOrAdd(string s)
    {
      int idx = strings.IndexOf(s);
      if (idx != -1) return idx;
      else
      {
        strings.Add(s);
        return strings.Count - 1;
      }
    }
```

```
  names = fullName.Split(' ').Select(getOrAdd).ToArray();
}

public string FullName => string.Join(" ", names.Select(i =>
strings[i]));
}
```

As you can see, the actual strings are stored in a single List. The full name, as it is fed into the constructor, is split into the constituent parts. Each part gets inserted (unless it is already there) into the list of strings, and the names array simply stores the indexes of the names in the list, however many there are. This means that, strings notwithstanding, the amount of nonstatic memory User2 takes up is 64 bits (two Int32s).

Now is a good time to pause and explain where exactly the Flyweight is. Essentially, the Flyweight is the index that we are storing. A Flyweight is a tiny object with a very small memory footprint that points to something larger that is stored elsewhere.

The only question remaining is whether or not this approach actually makes sense. Although it is very difficult to simulate this on actual users (this would require a live data set), we are going to do the following:

- Generate 100 first and 100 last names as random strings. The algorithm for making a random string is as follows:

```
public static string RandomString()
{
  Random rand = new Random();
  return new string(
    Enumerable.Range(0, 10)
            .Select(i => (char) ('a' + rand.
            Next(26))).ToArray());
}
```

- Next up, we make a concatenation (cross-product) of every first and last name and initialize 100 × 100 users:

```
var users = new List(); // or User2
foreach (var firstName in firstNames)
foreach (var lastName in lastNames)
  users.Add(new User($"{firstName} {lastName}"));
```

- Just to be safe, we force GC at this point.

- Finally, we use the dotMemory unit testing API to output the total amount of memory taken up by the program.

Running this entirely unscientific (but indicative) test on my machine tells me that the User2 implementation saves us 329,305 bytes. Is this significant? Well, let's calculate: a single ten-character string takes up 34 bytes (14 bytes[1] + 2 × 10 bytes for the letters), so 340,000 bytes for all the strings. This means we reduced the amount of memory taken by 97 percent! If this isn't cause for celebration, I don't know what is.

Text Formatting

Let's say you are working with a text editor, and you want to add formatting to text—for example, make text bold, make text italic, or capitalize it. How would you do this? One option is to treat each character individually: if your text is composed of X characters, you make a bool array of size X and simply flip each of the flags if you want to alter text. This would lead to the following implementation:

```
public class FormattedText
{
  private string plainText;
```

---

[1]The size of a string actually depends on the bitness of the operating system as well as the version of .NET that you are using.

```
public FormattedText(string plainText)
{
  this.plainText = plainText;
  capitalize = new bool[plainText.Length];
}

public void Capitalize(int start, int end)
{
  for (int i = start; i <= end; ++i)
    capitalize[i] = true;
}

private bool[] capitalize;
}
```

I am using capitalization here (because that's what a text console can render), but you can think of other forms of formatting being here, too. For every type of formatting, you would be making another Boolean array, initializing it to the right size in the constructor (and imagine the nightmare if the text changes), and then, of course, you would need to take into account those Boolean flags whenever you actually want to show the text somewhere:

```
public override string ToString()
{
  var sb = new StringBuilder();
  for (var i = 0; i < plainText.Length; i++)
  {
    var c = plainText[i];
    sb.Append(capitalize[i] ? char.ToUpper(c) : c);
  }
  return sb.ToString();
}
```

This approach does in fact work:

```
var ft = new FormattedText("This is a brave new world");
ft.Capitalize(10, 15);
WriteLine(ft); // This is a BRAVE new world
```

Of course, we are wasting memory. Even if the text has no formatting whatsoever, we still allocated the array. True, we could have made it lazy so that it is only created whenever someone uses the Capitalize() method, but then we would still lose a lot of memory on first use, particularly with large texts.

This is precisely the situation for which the Flyweight design pattern is made. In this particular case, we're going to define a Flyweight as a Range class that stores information about the start and end position of a substring within a string, as well as all the formatting information we desire:

```
public class TextRange
{
  public int Start, End;
  public bool Capitalize; // also Bold, Italic, etc.

  public bool Covers(int position)
  {
    return position >= Start && position <= End;
  }
}
```

Now, we can define a BetterFormattedText class that simply stores a list of all the formatting that was applied:

```
public class BetterFormattedText
{
  private readonly string plainText;
  private readonly List<TextRange> formatting
    = new List<TextRange>();
```

```
public BetterFormattedText(string plainText)
{
  this.plainText = plainText;
}

public TextRange GetRange(int start, int end)
{
  var range = new TextRange {Start = start, End = end};
  formatting.Add(range);
  return range;
}

public class TextRange { ... }
}
```

Notice that TextRange is an inner class—this is a design decision, and you could easily keep it external. Now, instead of a dedicated Capitalize() method, we simply have a method called GetRange() that does three things: It creates a new range, adds it to a list of formatting, and also returns it to the client to be operated on.

All that remains now is to make a new implementation of ToString() that incorporates this Flyweight-based approach. Here it is:

```
public override string ToString()
{
  var sb = new StringBuilder();

  for (var i = 0; i < plainText.Length; i++)
  {
    var c = plainText[i];
    foreach (var range in formatting)
      if (range.Covers(i) && range.Capitalize)
        c = char.ToUpperInvariant(c);
    sb.Append(c);
  }
```

175

```
    return sb.ToString();
}
```

As you can see, we simply iterate each of the characters. For each character, we check all the ranges with the `Covers()` method, and if that range covers this point and has special formatting, we show that formatting to the end user. Here is how you would use the new API:

```
var bft = new BetterFormattedText("This is a brave new world");
bft.GetRange(10, 15).Capitalize = true;
WriteLine(bft); // This is a BRAVE new world
```

Admittedly, ours is a fairly inefficient implementation of Flyweight (traversal of every character is just too tedious), but hopefully it is obvious that the general approach saves a lot of memory in the long run. A much faster implementation is clearly possible here, and is left as an exercise for the reader.

Summary

The Flyweight pattern is fundamentally a space-saving technique. Its exact incarnations are diverse: sometimes you have the Flyweight being returned as an API token that allows you to perform modifications of whoever has spawned it, whereas at other times the Flyweight is implicit, hiding behind the scenes, as in the case of our `User`, where the client isn't meant to know about the Flyweight actually being used.

In the .NET Framework, the principal Flyweight-like object is, of course, `Span<T>`. Just like the `TextRange` we implemented when working with strings, `Span<T>` is a type that has information about a part of an array: the starting position and length. Operations on the `Span` get applied to the object to which the `Span` refers, and .NET provides a rich API for creating spans on different types of objects. `Span` also makes heavy use of C# 7's `ref`-related APIs (e.g., `ref` returns).

CHAPTER 13

Proxy

When we looked at the Decorator design pattern, we saw the different ways of enhancing the functionality of an object. The Proxy design pattern is similar, but its goal is generally to preserve exactly (or as closely as possible) the API that is being used while offering certain internal enhancements.

Proxy is an unusual design pattern in that it isn't really homogeneous. The many different kinds of proxies people build are quite numerous and serve entirely different purposes. In this chapter we take a look at a selection of different proxy objects, and you can find more online.

Protection Proxy

The idea of a protection proxy, as the name suggests, is to provide access control to an existing object. For example, you might be starting out with an object called `Car` that has a single `Drive()` method that lets you drive the car (here we go, another synthetic example).

```
public class Car // : ICar
{
  public void Drive()
  {
    WriteLine("Car being driven");
  }
}
```

© Dmitri Nesteruk 2019
D. Nesteruk, *Design Patterns in .NET*, https://doi.org/10.1007/978-1-4842-4366-4_13

Later on, though, you decide that you want to only let people drive the car if they are old enough. What if you don't want to change Car itself and you want the extra checks to be done somewhere else (SRP)? First, you extract the ICar interface (note this operation doesn't affect Car in any significant way):

```
public interface ICar
{
  void Drive();
}
```

The protection Proxy we're going to build is going to depend on a Driver that is defined like this:

```
public class Driver
{
  public int Age { get; set; }

  public Driver(int age)
  {
    Age = age;
  }
}
```

The Proxy itself is going to take a Driver in the constructor and it's going to expose the same ICar interface as the original car, the only difference being that some internal checks occur to make sure the driver is old enough:

```
public class CarProxy : ICar
{
  private Car car = new Car();
  private Driver driver;
```

```
public CarProxy(Driver driver)
{
  this.driver = driver;
}

public void Drive()
{
  if (driver.Age >= 16)
    car.Drive();
  else
  {
    WriteLine("Driver too young");
  }
}
}
```

Here is how one would use this proxy:

```
ICar car = new CarProxy(new Driver(12));
car.Drive(); // Driver too young
```

There's one piece of the puzzle that we haven't really addressed. Even though both Car and CarProxy implement ICar, their constructors are not identical! This means that, strictly speaking, the interfaces of the two objects are not strictly identical. Is this a problem? This depends:

- If your code was dependent on Car rather than ICar (violating DIP), then you would need to search for and replace every use of this type in your code. That is not impossible with tools like ReSharper or Rider, just really annoying.

- If your code was dependent on ICar but you were explicitly invoking Car constructors, you would have to find all those constructor invocations and feed each of them a Driver.

- If you were using dependency injection, you are good
  to go provided you register a `Driver` in the container.

So, among other things, the protection proxy we've built is an
illustration of the benefits of using an IoC container with constructor
injection support.

Property Proxy

C# makes the use of properties easy: you can use either full or automatic
properties, and now there's expression-based notation for getters and
setters, so you can keep properties really concise. However, that's not
always what you want. Sometimes, you want a getter or setter of each
property in your code to do something in addition to just the default
actions. For example, you might want setters that prevent self-assignment
and also (for illustrative purposes) output some info about what value is
being assigned and to what property.

So instead of using ordinary properties, you might want to introduce
a *property proxy*—a class that, for all intents and purposes, behaves like a
property but is actually a separate class with domain-specific behaviors
(and associated performance costs). You would start building this class by
wrapping a simple value and adding whatever extra information you want
the property to have (e.g., the property name):

```csharp
public class Property<T> where T : new()
{
  private T value;
  private readonly string name;

  public T Value
  {
    get => value;
```

```
  set
  {
    if (Equals(this.value, value)) return;
    Console.WriteLine($"Assigning {value} to {name}");
    this.value = value;
  }
}

public Property() : this(default(T)) {}

public Property(T value, string name = "")
{
  this.value = value;
  this.name = name;
}
}
```

For now, all we have is a simple wrapper, but where's the *proxy* part of it all? After all, we want a Property<int> to behave as close to an int as possible. To that end, we can define a couple of implicit conversion operators:

```
public static implicit operator T(Property<T> property)
{
  return property.Value; // int n = p_int;
}

public static implicit operator Property<T>(T value)
{
  return new Property<T>(value); // Property<int> p = 123;
}
```

The first operator lets us implicitly convert the property type to its underlying value, and the second operator lets us initialize a property from a value (without a name, of course). Sadly, C# does not allow us to override the assignment = operator.

How would you use this property Proxy? Well, there are two ways I can think of. The most obvious is to expose the property as a public field.

```
public class Creature
{
  public Property<int> Agility
    = new Property<int>(10, nameof(Agility))
}
```

Unfortunately, this approach is not a "proper" Proxy because, although it replicates the interface of an ordinary property, it doesn't give us the behavior we want:

```
var c = new Creature();
c.Agility = 12; // <nothing happens!>
```

When you assign a value, as you would with an ordinary property, absolutely nothing happens. Why? Well, the reason is that we invoked the implicit conversion operator, which, instead of changing an existing property, just gave us a new property instead! That is definitely not what we wanted and, furthermore, we've lost the name value as it was never propagated by the operator.

The solution here, if we really want the property to both look like a duck and quack like a duck, is to create a wrapper (delegating) property, and keep the Proxy as a private backing field:

```
public class Creature
{
  public readonly Property<int> agility
    = new Property<int>(10, nameof(agility));
```

```
public int Agility
{
  get => agility.Value;
  set => agility.Value = value;
}
}
```

With this approach, we finally get the desired behavior:

```
var c = new Creature();
c.Agility = 12; // Assigning 12 to Agility
```

Purists might argue that this isn't an ideal Proxy (because we've had to both generate a new class and rewrite an existing property), but this is purely a limitation of the C# programming language.

Virtual Proxy

There are situations where you only want the object constructed when it is accessed, and you don't want to allocate it prematurely. If this was your starting strategy, you would typically use a Lazy<T> or similar mechanism, feeding the initialization code into its constructor lambda. However, there are situations when you are adding lazy instantiation at a later point in time, and you cannot change the existing API.

In this situation, what you end up building is a *virtual Proxy*: an object that has the same API as the original, giving the appearance of an instantiated object, but behind the scenes the Proxy only instantiates the object when it is actually necessary.

Imagine a typical image interface:

```
interface IImage
{
  void Draw();
}
```

An eager (opposite of lazy) implementation of a `Bitmap` (nothing to do with `System.Drawing.Bitmap`) would load the image from a file on construction, even if that image isn't actually required for anything. The following code is an emulation.

```csharp
class Bitmap : IImage
{
  private readonly string filename;

  public Bitmap(string filename)
  {
    this.filename = filename;
    WriteLine($"Loading image from {filename}");
  }

  public void Draw()
  {
    WriteLine($"Drawing image {filename}");
  }
}
```

The very act of construction of this `Bitmap` will trigger the loading of the image:

```csharp
var img = new Bitmap("pokemon.png");
// Loading image from pokemon.png
```

That's not quite what we want. We want the kind of bitmap that only loads itself when the `Draw()` method is used. Now, I suppose we could jump back into `Bitmap` and make it lazy, but we are going to assume the original implementation is set in stone and is not modifiable.

We can then build a virtual proxy that will use the original `Bitmap`, provide an identical interface, and also reuse the original `Bitmap`'s functionality:

```
class LazyBitmap : IImage
{
  private readonly string filename;
  private Bitmap bitmap;

  public LazyBitmap(string filename)
  {
    this.filename = filename;
  }

  public void Draw()
  {
    if (bitmap == null)
      bitmap = new Bitmap(filename);

    bitmap.Draw();
  }
}
```

Here we are. As you can see, the constructor of this LazyBitmap is a lot less "heavy": all it does is store the name of the file to load the image from, and that's it—the image doesn't actually get loaded.[1]

All of the magic happens in Draw(): This is where we check the bitmap reference to see whether the underlying (eager!) bitmap has been constructed. If it hasn't, we construct it, and then call its Draw() function to actually draw the image.

---

[1]Not that it matters for this particular example, but this implementation is not thread-safe. Imagine two threads that both do a null check, pass it, and then both assign bitmap one after another—the constructor will be called twice. This is why we use System.Lazy, which is thread-safe by design.

Now imagine you have some API that uses an IImage type:

```
public static void DrawImage(IImage img)
{
  WriteLine("About to draw the image");
  img.Draw();
  WriteLine("Done drawing the image");
}
```

We can use that API with an instance of LazyBitmap instead of Bitmap (hooray, polymorphism!) to render the image, loading it in a lazy fashion:

```
var img = new LazyBitmap("pokemon.png");
DrawImage(img); // image loaded here

// About to draw the image
// Loading image from pokemon.png
// Drawing image pokemon.png
// Done drawing the image
```

Communication Proxy

Suppose you call a method Foo() on an object of type Bar. Your typical assumption is that Bar has been allocated on the same machine as the one running your code, and you similarly expect Bar.Foo() to execute in the same process.

Now imagine that you make a design decision to move Bar and all its members to a different machine on the network, but you still want the old code to work. If you want to keep going as before, you need a *Communication Proxy*—a component that proxies the calls "over the wire" and of course collects results, if necessary.

Let's implement a simple ping-pong service to illustrate this. First, we define an interface:

```
interface IPingable
{
  string Ping(string message);
}
```

If we are building ping-pong in process, we can implement Pong as follows:

```
class Pong : IPingable
{
  public string Ping(string message)
  {
    return message + "pong";
  }
}
```

Basically, you ping a Pong and it appends the word "pong" to the end of the message and returns that message. Notice that I am not using a StringBuilder here, but instead making a new string on each turn: This lack of mutation helps replicate this API as a web service.

We can now try this setup and see how it works in process:

```
void UseIt(IPingable pp)
{
  WriteLine(pp.ping("ping"));
}

Pong pp = new Pong();
for (int i = 0; i < 3; ++i)
{
  UseIt(pp);
}
```

The end result is that we print "ping pong" three times, just as we wanted.

Now, suppose you decide to relocate the Pingable service to a web server, far, far away. Perhaps you even decide to expose it through a special framework such as ASP.NET:

```
[Route("api/[controller]")]
public class PingPongController : Controller
{
  [HttpGet("{msg}")]
  public string Get(string msg)
  {
    return msg + "pong";
  }
}
```

With this setup, we'll build a Communication Proxy called RemotePong that will be used in place of Pong.

```
class RemotePong : IPingable
{
  string Ping(string message)
  {
    string uri = "http://localhost:9149/api/pingpong/" + message;
    return new WebClient().DownloadString(uri);
  }
}
```

With this implemented, we can now make a single change:

```
RemotePong pp; // was Pong
for (int i = 0; i < 3; ++i)
{
  UseIt(pp);
}
```

That's it, you get the same output, but the actual implementation can be running on Kestrel in a Docker container somewhere halfway around the world.

Summary

This chapter has presented a number of proxies. Unlike the Decorator pattern, the Proxy doesn't try to expand the public API surface of an object by adding new members (unless it can't be helped). All it tries to do is enhance the underlying behavior of existing members.

Plenty of different Proxies exist:

- Property Proxies are stand-in objects that can replace fields and perform additional operations during assignment, access, or both.

- Virtual Proxies provide virtual access to the underlying object, and can implement behaviors such as lazy object loading. You might feel like you're working with a real object, but the underlying implementation might not have been created yet, and can, for example, be loaded on demand.

- Communication Proxies allow us to change the physical location of the object (e.g., move it to the cloud) but allow us to use pretty much the same API. Of course, in this case the API is just a shim for a remote service such as a REST API.

- Logging Proxies allow you to perform logging in addition to calling the underlying functions.

There are lots of other Proxies out there, and chances are that the ones you build yourself will not fall into a preexisting category, but will instead perform some action specific to your domain.

PART IV

Behavioral Patterns

When most people hear about behavioral patterns, it's mainly in relation to animals and how to get them to do what you want. Well, in a way, all of coding is about programs doing what you want, so behavioral software design patterns cover a very wide range of behaviors that are, nonetheless, quite common in programming.

As an example, consider the domain of software engineering. We have languages that are compiled, which involves lexing, parsing, and a million other things (the Interpreter pattern). Having constructed an abstract syntax tree (AST) for a program, you might want to analyze the program for possible bugs (the Visitor pattern). All of these are behaviors that are common enough to be expressed as patterns, and this is why we are here today.

Unlike Creational patterns (which are concerned exclusively with the creation of objects) or Structural patterns (which are concerned with composition, aggregation, and inheritance of objects), Behavioral design patterns do not follow a central theme. Although there are certain similarities between different patterns (e.g., Strategy and Template Method do the same thing in different ways), most patterns present unique approaches to solving a particular problem.

CHAPTER 14

Chain of Responsibility

Consider the typical example of corporate malpractice, insider trading. Say a particular trader has been caught red-handed trading on inside information. Who is to blame for this? If management didn't know, it's the trader. Maybe the trader's peers were in on it, though, in which case the group manager might be the one responsible. Perhaps the practice is institutional, in which case the CEO would take the blame.[1]

This is an example of a responsibility chain: You have several different elements of a system that can all process a message one after another. As a concept, it is rather easy to implement, because all that's implied is the use of a list.

Scenario

Imagine a computer game where each creature has a name and two characteristic values, Attack and Defense:

---

[1]In all likelihood, if we're talking about banking, nobody gets punished. Nobody was punished for the subprime mortgage crisis. In the LIBOR fixing scandal only one trader got convicted (six bankers were accused in the United Kingdom but later cleared). What does this have to do with design patterns? Absolutely nothing! I just wanted to share.

```
public class Creature
{
  public string Name;
  public int Attack, Defense;

  public Creature(string name, int attack, int defense) { ... }
}
```

Now, as the creature progresses through the game, it might pick up an item (e.g., a magic sword), or it might end up getting enchanted. In either case, its attack and defense values will be modified by something we call a CreatureModifier.

Furthermore, situations where several modifiers are applied are not uncommon, so we need to be able to stack modifiers on top of a creature, allowing them to be applied in the order in which they were attached. Let's see how we can implement this.

Method Chain

In the classic Chain of Responsibility implementation, we define CreatureModifier as follows:

```
public class CreatureModifier
{
  protected Creature creature;
  protected CreatureModifier next;

  public CreatureModifier(Creature creature)
  {
    this.creature = creature;
  }

  public void Add(CreatureModifier cm)
  {
```

```
  if (next != null) next.Add(cm);
  else next = cm;
}
public virtual void Handle() => next?.Handle();
}
```

There are a lot of things happening here, so let's discuss them in turn:

- The class takes and stores a reference to the Creature it plans to modify.

- The class doesn't really do much, but it is not abstract: All its members have implementations. The next member points to an optional CreatureModifier following this one. The implication is, of course, that the modifier can also be some inheritor of CreatureModifier.

- The Add() method adds another creature modifier to the modifier chain. This is done iteratively: If the current modifier is null we set it to that, otherwise we traverse the entire chain and put it on the end. Naturally this traversal has $O(n)$ complexity.

- The Handle() method simply handles the next item in the chain, if it exists; it has no behavior of its own. The fact that it's virtual implies that it is meant to be overridden.

So far, all we have is an implementation of a poor man's append-only singly linked list. When we start inheriting from it, though, things will hopefully become clearer. For example, here is how you would make a modifier that would double the creature's attack value:

```
public class DoubleAttackModifier : CreatureModifier
{
  public DoubleAttackModifier(Creature creature)
    : base(creature) {}
```

195

```csharp
public override void Handle()
{
  WriteLine($"Doubling {creature.Name}'s attack");
  creature.Attack *= 2;
  base.Handle();
}
}
```

Finally we are getting somewhere. This modifier inherits from
CreatureModifier, and in its Handle() method does two things: doubles
the attack value and calls Handle() from the base class. That second part
is critical: The only way in which a *chain* of modifiers can be applied
is if every inheritor doesn't forget to call the base at the end of its own
Handle() implementation.

Here is another, more complicated modifier. This modifier increases
the defense of creatures with attack of 2 or less by 1:

```csharp
public class IncreaseDefenseModifier : CreatureModifier
{
  public IncreaseDefenseModifier(Creature creature)
    : base(creature) {}

  public override void Handle()
  {
    if (creature.Attack <= 2)
    {
      WriteLine($"Increasing {creature.Name}'s defense");
      creature.Defense++;
    }

    base.Handle();
  }
}
```

Again we call the base class at the end. Putting it all together, we can now make a creature and apply a combination of modifiers to it:

```
var goblin = new Creature("Goblin", 1, 1);
WriteLine(goblin); // Name: Goblin, Attack: 1, Defense: 1

var root = new CreatureModifier(goblin);
root.Add(new DoubleAttackModifier(goblin));
root.Add(new DoubleAttackModifier(goblin));
root.Add(new IncreaseDefenseModifier(goblin));

// eventually...
root.Handle();
WriteLine(goblin); // Name: Goblin, Attack: 4, Defense: 1
```

As you can see, this goblin is a 4/1 because its attack got doubled and the defense modifier, although added, did not affect its defense score.

Here's another curious point. Suppose you decide to cast a spell on a creature such that no bonus can be applied to it. Is it easy to do? Quite easy, actually, because all you have to do is avoid calling the base Handle(): This avoids executing the entire chain:

```
public class NoBonusesModifier : CreatureModifier
{
  public NoBonusesModifier(Creature creature)
    : base(creature) {}

  public override void Handle()
  {
    WriteLine("No bonuses for you!");
    // no call to base.Handle() here
  }
}
```

That's it! Now, if you slot the NoBonusesModifier at the beginning of the chain, no further elements will be applied.

Broker Chain

The example with the pointer chain is very artificial. In the real world, you would want creatures to be able to take on and lose bonuses arbitrarily, something that an append-only linked list doesn't support. Furthermore, you don't want to modify the underlying creature stats permanently (as we did); instead, you want to keep modifications temporary.

One way to implement Chain of Responsibility is through a centralized component. This component can keep a list of all modifiers available in the game, and can facilitate queries for a particular creature's attack or defense by ensuring that all relevant bonuses are applied.

The component that we are going to build is called an *event broker*. Because it is connected to every participating component it represents the Mediator design pattern and, further, because it responds to queries through events, it leverages the Observer design pattern.

Let's build one. First, we define a structure called Game that will represent a game that's being played:

```
public class Game // mediator pattern
{
  public event EventHandler<Query> Queries; // effectively a chain

  public void PerformQuery(object sender, Query q)
  {
    Queries?.Invoke(sender, q);
  }
}
```

The class Game is what we generally call an *event broker*: a central component that brokers (passes) events between different parts of the system. Here it is implemented using ordinary .NET events, but you can equally imagine an implementation using some sort of message queue.

In the game, we are using an event called called Queries. Essentially, this lets us raise this event and have it handled by every subscriber (listening component). What do events have to do with querying a creature's attack or defense?

Imagine that you want to query a creature's statistic. You could certainly try to read a field, but remember, we need to apply all the modifiers before the final value is known. So instead we'll encapsulate a query in a separate object (this is the Command pattern[2]) defined as follows:

```
public class Query
{
  public string CreatureName;
  public enum Argument
  {
    Attack, Defense
  }
  public Argument WhatToQuery;
  public int Value; // bidirectional!
}
```

All we've done in this class is encapsulated the concept of querying a particular value from a creature. All we need to provide is the name of the creature and which statistic we're interested in. It is precisely this value

---

[2]Actually, there's a bit of confusion here. The concept of Command Query Separation (CQS) suggests the separation of operations into commands (which mutate state and yield no value) and queries (which do not mutate anything but yield a value). The GoF does not have a concept of a Query, so we let any encapsulated instruction to a component be called a Command.

(well, a reference to it) that will be constructed and used by Game.Queries to apply the modifiers and return the final Value.

Now, let's move on to the definition of Creature. It's very similar to what we had before. The only difference in terms of fields is a reference to a Game:

```
public class Creature
{
  private Game game;
  public string Name;
  private int attack, defense;

  public Creature(Game game, string name, int attack, int defense)
  {
    // obvious stuff here
  }
  // other members here
}
```

Now, notice how attack and defense are private fields. This means that, to get at the *final* (postmodifier) attack value you would need to call a separate read-only property; for example:

```
public int Attack
{
  get
  {
    var q = new Query(Name, Query.Argument.Attack, attack);
    game.PerformQuery(this, q);
    return q.Value;
  }
}
```

This is where the magic happens! Instead of just returning a value or statically applying some reference-based chain, what we do is create a Query with the right arguments and then send the query off to be handled by whoever is subscribed to Game.Queries. Every single listening component gets a chance to modify the baseline attack value.

So let's now implement the modifiers. Once again, we'll make a base class, but this time it won't have a body for the Handle() method:

```
public abstract class CreatureModifier : IDisposable
{
  protected Game game;
  protected Creature creature;

  protected CreatureModifier(Game game, Creature creature)
  {
    this.game = game;
    this.creature = creature;
    game.Queries += Handle; // subscribe
  }

  protected abstract void Handle(object sender, Query q);

  public void Dispose()
  {
    game.Queries -= Handle; // unsubscribe
  }
}
```

This time around, the CreatureModifier class is even more sophisticated. It obviously keeps a reference to the creature it is meant to modify, but also to the Game that is being played. Why? Well, as you can see, what is happening is that, in the constructor, it subscribes to the Queries event so that its inheritors can inject themselves as a set of modifiers is applied one after another. We also implement IDisposable so as to unsubscribe from the query events and prevent memory leaks.[3]

The CreatureModifier.Handle() method is deliberately made abstract so that inheritors can implement it and handle the modification process depending on the Query that is being sent. Let's take a look at how this is used by reimplementing DoubleCreatureModifier in this new paradigm:

```
public class DoubleAttackModifier : CreatureModifier
{
  public DoubleAttackModifier(Game game, Creature creature)
    : base(game, creature) {}

  protected override void Handle(object sender, Query q)
  {
    if (q.CreatureName == creature.Name &&
        q.WhatToQuery == Query.Argument.Attack)
      q.Value *= 2;
  }
}
```

Now we have a concrete implementation of Handle(). Extra care needs to be taken here to identify that the query is, in fact, a query that we want to process. Because a DoubleAttackModifier only cares about queries for an attack value, we verify this particular argument (WhatToQuery) and also make sure that the query is related to the creature we are meant to investigate.

If we now add an IncreaseDefenseModifier (increases defense by 2; implementation omitted) we can now run the following scenario:

```
var game = new Game();
var goblin = new Creature(game, "Strong Goblin", 2, 2);
WriteLine(goblin); // Name: Strong Goblin, attack: 2, defense: 2
```

---

[3]This is precisely what is done in Reactive Extensions. See Chapter 19 for more information.

```
using (new DoubleAttackModifier(game, goblin))
{
  WriteLine(goblin); // Name: Strong Goblin, attack: 4, defense: 2
  using (new IncreaseDefenseModifier(game, goblin))
  {
    WriteLine(goblin); // Name: Strong Goblin, attack: 4, defense: 4
  }
}

WriteLine(goblin); // Name: Strong Goblin, attack: 2, defense: 2
```

What is happening here? Well, prior to being modified, the goblin is a 2/2. Then, we manufacture a scope, within which the goblin is affected by a DoubleAttackModifier, so inside the scope, it is a 4/2 creature. As soon as we exit the scope, the modifier's destructor triggers and it disconnects itself from the broker and thus no longer affects the values when they are queried. Consequently, the goblin itself reverts to being a 2/2 creature once again.

Summary

Chain of Responsibility is a very simple design pattern that lets components process a command (or a query) in turn. The simplest implementation of Chain of Responsibility is one where you simply make a reference chain and, in theory, you could replace it with just an ordinary List or, perhaps, a LinkedList if you wanted fast removal as well.

A more sophisticated Broker Chain implementation that also leverages Mediator and Observer patterns allows us to process queries on an event, letting each subscriber perform modifications of the originally passed object (it is a single reference that goes through the entire chain) before the final values are returned to the client.

CHAPTER 15

Command

Think about a trivial variable assignment, such as meaningOfLife = 42. The variable got assigned, but there's no record anywhere that the assignment took place. Nobody can give us the previous value. We cannot take the *fact* of assignment and serialize it somewhere. This is problematic, because without a record of the change, we are unable to roll back to previous values, perform audits, or do history-based debugging.[1]

The Command design pattern proposes that, instead of working with objects directly by manipulating them through their APIs, we send them *commands,* or instructions on how to do something. A command is nothing more than a data class with its members describing what to do and how to do it. Let's take a look at a typical scenario.

Scenario

Let's try to model a typical bank account that has a balance and an overdraft limit. We'll implement Deposit() and Withdraw() methods on it:

```
public class BankAccount
{
  private int balance;
  private int overdraftLimit = -500;
```

---

[1]We do have dedicated historical debugging tools such as Microsoft Visual Studio's IntelliTrace or UndoDB.

© Dmitri Nesteruk 2019
D. Nesteruk, *Design Patterns in .NET*, https://doi.org/10.1007/978-1-4842-4366-4_15

```
public void Deposit(int amount)
{
  balance += amount;
  WriteLine($"Deposited ${amount}, balance is now {balance}");
}

public void Withdraw(int amount)
{
  if (balance - amount >= overdraftLimit)
  {
    balance -= amount;
    WriteLine($"Withdrew ${amount}, balance is now {balance}");
  }
}

public override string ToString()
{
  return $"{nameof(balance)}: {balance}";
}
}
```

Now we can call the methods directly, of course, but let us suppose that, for audit purposes, we need to make a record of every deposit and withdrawal made and we cannot do it right inside BankAccount because—guess what—we've already designed, implemented, and tested that class.[2]

Implementing the Command Pattern

We begin by defining an interface for a command.

---

[2]You can design your code in a Command-first fashion; that is, ensure that commands are the only publicly accessible API that your objects provide.

```
public interface ICommand
{
  void Call();
}
```

Having made the interface, we can now use it to define a BankAccountCommand that will encapsulate information about what to do with a bank account:

```
public class BankAccountCommand : ICommand
{
  private BankAccount account;
  public enum Action
  {
    Deposit, Withdraw
  }
  private Action action;
  private int amount;

  public BankAccountCommand
    (BankAccount account, Action action, int amount) { ... }
}
```

The information contained in the Command includes the following:

- The account on which to operate.

- The action to take; both the set of options and the variable to store the action are defined in the class.

- The amount to deposit or withdraw.

Once the client provides this information, we can take it and use it to perform the deposit or withdrawal:

```
public void Call()
{
  switch (action)
```

```
{
  case Action.Deposit:
    account.Deposit(amount);
    succeeded = true;
    break;
  case Action.Withdraw:
    succeeded = account.Withdraw(amount);
    break;
  default:
    throw new ArgumentOutOfRangeException();
  }
}
```

With this approach, we can create the Command and then perform modifications of the account right on the Command:

```
var ba = new BankAccount();
var cmd = new BankAccountCommand(ba,
  BankAccountCommand.Action.Deposit, 100);
cmd.Call(); // Deposited $100, balance is now 100
WriteLine(ba); // balance: 100
```

This will deposit $100 into our account. Easy! If you are worried that we are still exposing the original Deposit() and Withdraw() member functions to the client, the only way to hide them is to make Commands inner classes of the BankAccount itself.

Undo Operations

Because a Command encapsulates all information about some modification to a BankAccount, it can equally roll back this modification and return its target object to its prior state.

To begin with, we need to decide whether to stick undo-related operations into our Command interface. I do it here for purposes of brevity, but in general, this is a design decision that needs to respect the Interface Segregation Principle that we discussed at the beginning of the book. For example, if you envisage some commands being final and not subject to undo mechanics, it might make sense to split ICommand into, say, ICallable and IUndoable.

Here is the updated ICommand:

```
public interface ICommand
{
  void Call();
  void Undo();
}
```

Here is a naïve (but working) implementation of BankAccountCommand. Undo(), motivated by the (incorrect) assumption that Deposit() and Withdraw() are symmetric operations:

```
public void Undo()
{
  switch (action)
  {
    case Action.Deposit:
      account.Withdraw(amount);
      break;
    case Action.Withdraw:
      account.Deposit(amount);
      break;
    default:
      throw new ArgumentOutOfRangeException();
  }
}
```

Why is this implementation broken? Because if you tried to withdraw an amount equal to the gross domestic product of a developed nation, you would not be successful, but when rolling back the transaction, we don't have a way of telling that it failed!

To get this information, we modify withdraw() to return a success flag:

```csharp
public bool Withdraw(int amount)
{
  if (balance - amount >= overdraftLimit)
  {
    balance -= amount;
    Console.WriteLine($"Withdrew ${amount}, balance is now
    {balance}");
    return true; // succeeded
  }
  return false; // failed
}
```

That's much better. We can now modify the entire BankAccountCommand to do two things:

- Store internally a succeeded flag when a withdrawal is made. We assume that Deposit() cannot fail.

- Use this flag when Undo() is called.

Here we go:

```csharp
public class BankAccountCommand : ICommand
{
  ...
  private bool succeeded;
}
```

Now we have the flag, and we can improve our implementation of Undo():

```
public void Undo()
{
  if (!succeeded) return;
  switch (action)
  {
    case Action.Deposit:
      account.Deposit(amount); // assumed to always succeed
      succeeded = true;
      break;
    case Action.Withdraw:
      succeeded = account.Withdraw(amount);
      break;
    default:
      throw new ArgumentOutOfRangeException();
  }
}
```

Now we can finally undo withdrawal commands in a consistent fashion.

```
var ba = new BankAccount();
var cmdDeposit = new BankAccountCommand(ba,
  BankAccountCommand.Action.Deposit, 100);
var cmdWithdraw = new BankAccountCommand(ba,
  BankAccountCommand.Action.Withdraw, 1000);
cmdDeposit.Call();
cmdWithdraw.Call();
WriteLine(ba); // balance: 100
cmdWithdraw.Undo();
cmdDeposit.Undo();
WriteLine(ba); // balance: 0
```

The goal of this exercise was, of course, to illustrate that in addition to storing information about the action to perform, a Command can also store some intermediate information that is, once again, useful for things like audits. If you detect a series of 100 failed withdrawal attempts, you can investigate a potential hack.

Composite Commands

A transfer of money from Account A to Account B can be simulated with two Commands:

1. Withdraw $X from A.

2. Deposit $X to B.

It would be nice if, instead of creating and calling these two Commands, we could just create and call a single Command that encapsulates both of them. This is the essence of the Composite design pattern that we discuss later.

Let's define a skeleton composite Command. I'm going to inherit from List<BankAccountCommand> and, of course, implement the ICommand interface:

```
abstract class CompositeBankAccountCommand :
List<BankAccountCommand>, ICommand
{
  public virtual void Call()
  {
    ForEach(cmd => cmd.Call());
  }

  public virtual void Undo()
  {
    foreach (var cmd in
```

```
    ((IEnumerable<BankAccountCommand>)this).Reverse())
  {
    cmd.Undo();
  }
 }
}
```

As you can see, the CompositeBankAccountCommand is both a list and a Command, which fits the definition of the Composite design pattern. I have implemented both Undo() and Redo() operations; note that the Undo() process goes through Commands in reverse order; hopefully I don't have to explain why you would want this as default behavior. The cast is there because a List<T> has its own, void-returning, mutating Reverse() that we definitely do not want. If you don't like what you see here, you can use a for loop or some other base type that doesn't do in-place reversal.

So now, how about a composite Command specifically for transferring money? I would define it as follows:

```
class MoneyTransferCommand : CompositeBankAccountCommand
{
  public MoneyTransferCommand(BankAccount from,
    BankAccount to, int amount)
  {
    AddRange(new []
    {
      new BankAccountCommand(from,
        BankAccountCommand.Action.Withdraw, amount),
      new BankAccountCommand(to,
        BankAccountCommand.Action.Deposit, amount)
    });
  }
}
```

As you can see, all we're doing is providing a constructor to initialize the object with. We keep reusing the base class `Undo()` and `Redo()` implementations.

But that's not right, is it? The base class implementations don't quite cut it because they don't incorporate the idea of failure. If I fail to withdraw money from A, I shouldn't deposit that money to B: The entire chain should cancel itself.

To support this idea, more drastic changes are required. We need to do the following:

- Add a `Success` flag to `Command`. This, of course, implies that we can no longer use an interface. We need an abstract class.

- Record the success or failure of every operation.

- Ensure that the command can only be undone if it originally succeeded.

- Introduce a new in-between class called `DependentCompositeCommand` that is very careful about actually rolling back the commands.

Let's assume that we've performed the refactoring such that `Command` is now an abstract class with a Boolean `Success` member; the `BankAccountCommand` now `overrides` both `Undo()` and `Redo()`.

When calling each command, we only do so if the previous one succeeded; otherwise we simply set the `success` flag to `false`.

```
public override void Call()
{
  bool ok = true;
  foreach (var cmd in this)
  {
    if (ok)
    {
```

```
    cmd.Call();
    ok = cmd.Success;
  }
  else
  {
    cmd.Success = false;
  }
 }
}
```

There is no need to override the Undo() because each of our Commands checks its own Success flag and undoes the operation only if it is set to true. Here is a scenario that demonstrates the correct operation of the new scheme when the source account doesn't have enough funds for the transfer to succeed.

```
var from = new BankAccount();
from.Deposit(100);
var to = new BankAccount();

var mtc = new MoneyTransferCommand(from, to, 1000);
mtc.Call();
WriteLine(from); // balance: 100
WriteLine(to);   // balance: 0
```

One can imagine an even stronger form of this scenario where a composite Command only succeeds if all of its parts succeed (think about a transfer where the withdrawal succeeds but the deposit fails because the account is locked; would you want it to go through?). This is a bit harder to implement, and I leave it as an exercise for the reader.

The entire purpose of this section was to illustrate how a simple Command-based approach can get quite complicated when real-world business requirements are taken into account. Whether or not you actually need this complexity is up to you.

Functional Command

The Command design pattern is typically implemented using classes. It is, however, possible to also implement this pattern in a functional way.

First of all, one might argue that an `ICommand` interface with a single `Call()` method is simply unnecessary: we already have delegates such as `Func` and `Action` that can serve as de facto interfaces for our purposes. Similarly, when it comes to invoking the Commands, we can invoke said delegates directly instead of calling a member of some interface.

Here is a trivial illustration of the approach. We begin by defining a `BankAccount` simply as:

```
public class BankAccount
{
  public int Balance;
}
```

We can then define different commands to operate on the bank account as independent methods. These could, alternatively, be packaged into ready-made function objects; there's no real difference between the two:

```
public void Deposit(BankAccount account, int amount)
{
  account.Balance += amount;
}

public void Withdraw(BankAccount account, int amount)
{
  if (account.Balance >= amount)
    account.Balance -= amount;
}
```

Every single method represents a Command. We can therefore bundle up the Commands in a simple list and process them one after another:

```
var ba = new BankAccount();
var commands = new List<Action>();

commands.Add(() => Deposit(ba, 100));
commands.Add(() => Withdraw(ba, 100));

commands.ForEach(c => c());
```

You might feel that this model is a great simplification of the one we had previously when talking about ICommand. After all, any invocation can be reduced to a parameterless Action that simply captures the needed elements in the lambda. However, this approach has significant downsides, namely:

- *Direct references:* A lambda that captures a specific object by necessity extends its lifetime. Although this is great in terms of correctness (you'll never invoke a Command with a nonexistent object), there are situations where you want commands to persist longer than the objects they need to affect.

- *Logging:* If you wanted to record every single action being performed on an account, you still need some sort of Command processor. How can you determine which Command is being invoked? All you are looking at is an Action or similarly nondescript delegate, so how do you determine whether it's a deposit or a withdrawal or something entirely different, like a composite Command?

- *Marshaling:* Quite simply, you cannot marshal a lambda. You could perhaps marshal an expression tree (as in, an Expression<Func<>>), but even then parsing expression trees is not the easiest thing to do. A conventional OOP-based approach is easier because a class can be deterministically (de)serialized.

- *Secondary operations:* Unlike functional objects, an OOP Command (or its interface) can define operations other than invocation. We've looked at examples such as Undo(), but other operations could include things like Log(), Print(), or something else. A functional approach doesn't give you this sort of flexibility.

To sum up, although the functional pattern does represent some action that needs to be done, it only encapsulates its principal behavior. A function is difficult to inspect or traverse, it is difficult to serialize, and if it captures context this has obvious lifetime implications. Use with caution!

Queries and Command Query Separation

The notion of Command Query Separation (CQS) is the idea that operations in a system fall broadly into the following two categories:

- Commands, which are instructions for the system to perform some operation that involves mutation of state, but yields no value.

- Queries, which are requests for information that yield values but do not mutate state.

The GoF book does not define a Query as a separate pattern, so to settle this issue once and for all, I propose the following, very simple, definition: A *query* is a special type of command that does not mutate state. Instead, a query instructs components to provide some information, such as a value calculated on the basis of interaction with one or more components.

There. We can now argue that both parts of CQS fall under the Command design pattern, the only difference being that queries have a return value—not in the return sense, of course, but rather in having a mutable field or property that any command processor can initialize or modify.

Summary

The Command design pattern is simple: it basically suggests that components can communicate with one another using special objects that encapsulate instructions, rather than specifying those same instructions as arguments to a method.

Sometimes, you don't want such an object to mutate the target or cause it to do something specific; instead you want to use such an object to get some information from the target, in which case we typically call such an object a Query. In most cases, a query is an immutable object that relies on the return type of the method, but there are situations (see, e.g., the Chain of Responsibility Broker Chain example) when you want the result that is being returned to be modified by other components. The components themselves are still not modified, however; only the result is.

Commands are used a lot in UI systems to encapsulate typical actions (e.g., copy or paste) and then allow a single command to be invoked by several different means. For example, you can copy by using the top-level application menu, a button on the toolbar, the context menu, or a keyboard shortcut.

Finally, these actions can be combined into composite Commands (macros)—sequences of actions that can be recorded and then replayed at will. Notice that a composite Command can also be composed of other composite Commands (as per the Composite design pattern).

CHAPTER 16

Interpreter

> Any good software engineer will tell you that a compiler and an interpreter are interchangeable.
>
> —Tim Berners-Lee

The goal of the Interpreter design pattern is—you guessed it—to interpret input, particularly *textual* input, although to be fair it really doesn't matter what type. The notion of an Interpreter is greatly linked to Compiler Theory and similar courses taught at universities. Because we don't have nearly enough space here to delve into the complexities of different types of parsers and whatnot, the purpose of this chapter is to simply show some examples of the kinds of things you might want to interpret. Here are a few fairly obvious ones:

- Numeric literals such as `42` or `1.234e12` need to be interpreted to be stored efficiently in binary. In C#, these operations are covered via methods such as `Int.Parse()`.[1]

---

[1] The parsing of numbers is the top operation that gets redefined (optimized) by developers of algorithmic trading systems. The default implementations are very powerful and can handle many different number formats, but in real life the stock market typically feeds you data with uniform precision and notation, allowing the construction of much faster (orders of magnitude) parsers.

© Dmitri Nesteruk 2019
D. Nesteruk, *Design Patterns in .NET*, https://doi.org/10.1007/978-1-4842-4366-4_16

- Regular expressions help us find patterns in text, but what you need to realize is that regular expressions are essentially a separate, embedded, domain-specific language (DSL). Naturally, before using them, they must be interpreted correctly.

- Any structured data, be it CSV, XML, JSON, or something more complicated, requires interpretation before it can be used.

- At the pinnacle of the application of Interpreter, we have fully fledged programming languages. After all, a compiler or interpreter for a language like C or Python must actually understand the language before compiling something executable.

Given the proliferation and diversity of challenges related to interpretation, we simply look at some examples. These serve to illustrate how one can build an Interpreter, either making one from scratch or using a specialized library or parser framework.

Numeric Expression Evaluator

Let's imagine that we decide to parse *very* simple mathematical expressions such as 3 + (5 - 4); that is, we restrict ourselves to addition, subtraction, and parentheses. We want a program that can read such an expression and, of course, calculate the expression's final value.

We are going to build the calculator by hand, without resorting to any parsing framework. This should hopefully highlight some of the complexity involved in parsing textual input.

Lexing

The first step to interpreting an expression is called *lexing*, and it involves turning a sequence of characters into a sequence of *tokens*. A token is typically a primitive syntactic element, and we should end up with a flat sequence of these. In our case, a token can be

- An integer.

- An operator (plus or minus).

- An opening or closing parenthesis.

Thus, we can define the following structure:

```
public class Token
{
  public enum Type
  {
    Integer, Plus, Minus, Lparen, Rparen
  }

  public Type MyType;
  public string Text;

  public Token(Type type, string text)
  {
    MyType = type;
    Text = text;
  }

  public override string ToString()
  {
    return $"`{Text}`";
  }
}
```

You'll note that Token is not an enum because, apart from the type, we also want to store the text that this token relates to, as it is not always predefined. (We could, alternatively, store some Range that would refer to the original string.)

Now, given a string containing an expression, we can define a lexing process that will turn text into a List<Token>:

```
static List<Token> Lex(string input)
{
  var result = new List<Token>();

  for (int i = 0; i < input.Length; i++)
  {
    switch (input[i])
    {
      case '+':
        result.Add(new Token(Token.Type.Plus, "+"));
        break;
      case '-':
        result.Add(new Token(Token.Type.Minus, "-"));
        break;
      case '(':
        result.Add(new Token(Token.Type.Lparen, "("));
        break;
      case ')':
        result.Add(new Token(Token.Type.Rparen, ")"));
        break;
      default:
        // todo
    }
  }
}
```

```
    return result;
}
```

Parsing predefined tokens is easy. In fact, we could have added them as a

```
Dictionary<BinaryOperation.Type, char>
```

to simplify things. Parsing a number is not so easy, though. If we hit a 1, we should wait and see what the next character is. For this we define a separate routine:

```
var sb = new StringBuilder(input[i].ToString());
for (int j = i + 1; j < input.Length; ++j)
{
  if (char.IsDigit(input[j]))
  {
    sb.Append(input[j]);
    ++i;
  }
  else
  {
    result.Add(new Token(Token.Type.Integer, sb.ToString()));
    break;
  }
}
```

Essentially, while we keep reading (pumping) digits, we add them to the buffer. When we're done, we make a Token out of the entire buffer and add it to the resulting list.

Parsing

The process of *parsing* turns a sequence of tokens into meaningful, typically object-oriented, structures. At the top, it is often useful to have an abstract class or interface that all elements of the tree implement:

```
public interface IElement
{
  int Value { get; }
}
```

The type's Value evaluates this element's numeric value. Next, we can create an element for storing integral values (e.g., 1, 5, or 42):

```
public class Integer : IElement
{
  public Integer(int value)
  {
    Value = value;
  }

  public int Value { get; }
}
```

If we don't have an Integer, we must have an operation such as addition or subtraction. In our case, all operations are *binary*, meaning they have two parts. For example, 2 + 3 in our model can be represented in pseudocode as BinaryOperation{Literal{2}, Literal{3}, addition}:

```
public class BinaryOperation : IElement
{
  public enum Type
```

```
{
  Addition,
  Subtraction
}

public Type MyType;
public IElement Left, Right;

public int Value
{
  get
  {
    switch (MyType)
    {
      case Type.Addition:
        return Left.Value + Right.Value;
      case Type.Subtraction:
        return Left.Value - Right.Value;
      default:
        throw new ArgumentOutOfRangeException();
    }
  }
}
}
```

On to the parsing process. All we need to do is turn a sequence of Tokens into a binary tree of IExpressions. From the outset, it can look as follows:

```
static IElement Parse(IReadOnlyList<Token> tokens)
{
  var result = new BinaryOperation();
  bool haveLHS = false;
  for (int i = 0; i < tokens.Count; i++)
```

```
  {
    var token = tokens[i];

    // look at the type of token
    switch (token.MyType)
    {
      // process each token in turn
    }
  }
  return result;
}
```

The only thing we need to discuss from this code is the haveLHS variable. Remember, we are trying to get a tree, and at the *root* of that tree we expect a BinaryExpression, which, by definition, has left and right sides. When we are on a number, though, how do we know if it is the left or right side of an expression? We don't, which is why we track this using haveLHS.

Now let's go through these case by case. First, integers map directly to our Integer construct, so all we have to do is turn text into a number. (Incidentally, we could have also done this at the lexing stage if we wanted to.)

```
case Token.Type.Integer:
  var integer = new Integer(int.Parse(token.Text));
  if (!haveLHS)
  {
    result.Left = integer;
    haveLHS = true;
  } else
  {
    result.Right = integer;
  }
  break;
```

The plus and minus tokens simply determine the type of operation we're currently processing, so they are easy:

```
case Token.Type.Plus:
  result.MyType = BinaryOperation.Type.Addition;
  break;
case Token.Type.Minus:
  result.MyType = BinaryOperation.Type.Subtraction;
  break;
```

Then there's the left parenthesis. Yep, just the left, we don"t detect the right one explicitly. Basically, the idea here is simple: Find the closing right parenthesis (I'm ignoring nested brackets for now), rip out the entire subexpression, Parse() it recursively, and set as the left or right side of the expression we are currently working with:

```
case Token.Type.Lparen:
  int j = i;
  for (; j < tokens.Count; ++j)
    if (tokens[j].MyType == Token.Type.Rparen)
      break; // found it!
  // process subexpression w/o opening
  var subexpression = tokens.Skip(i+1).Take(j - i - 1).ToList();
  var element = Parse(subexpression);
  if (!haveLHS)
  {
    result.Left = element;
    haveLHS = true;
  } else result.Right = element;
  i = j; // advance
  break;
```

In a real-world scenario, you would want a lot more safety features in here: not just handling nested parentheses (which I think is a must), but handling incorrect expressions where the closing parenthesis is missing. If it is indeed missing, how would you handle it? Throw an exception? Try to parse whatever is left and assume the closing is at the very end? Something else? All of these issues are left as an exercise for the reader.

Using Lexer and Parser

With both Lex() and Parse() implemented, we can finally parse the expression and calculate its value:

```
var input = "(13+4)-(12+1)";
var tokens = Lex(input);
WriteLine(string.Join("\t", tokens));
// `(`  `13`  `+`  `4`  `)`  `-`  `(`  `12`  `+`  `1`  `)`

var parsed = Parse(tokens);
WriteLine($"{input} = {parsed.Value}");
// (13-4)-(12+1) = -4
```

Interpretation in the Functional Paradigm

If you look at a set of elements that are produced by either the lexing or the parsing process, you will quickly see that they are trivial structures that would map very neatly onto F#'s discriminated unions. This, in turn, allows us to subsequently use pattern matching when there comes a time to traverse a (recursive) discriminated union to transform it into something else.

Here's an example: Suppose you are given a definition of a mathematical expression and you want to print or evaluate it.[2] Let's define the structure in XML so we don't have to go through a difficult parsing process:

```
<math>
  <plus>
    <value>2</value>
    <value>3</value>
  </plus>
</math>
```

We can create a recursive discriminated union to represent this structure:

```
type Expression =
  Math of Expression list
  | Plus of lhs:Expression * rhs:Expression
  | Value of value:string
```

As you can see, there is a one-to-one correspondence between the XML elements and the corresponding Expression cases (e.g., <math> → Math). To instantiate cases, we would need to use reflection. One trick I adopt here is to precompute the case constructors using APIs from the Microsoft.FSharp.Reflection namespace:

```
let cases = FSharpType.GetUnionCases (typeof<Expression>)
            |> Array.map(fun f ->
               (f.Name, FSharpValue.PreComputeUnionConstructor(f)))
            |> Map.ofArray
```

---

[2]This is a small illustration of something that's a real-life commercial product called MathSharp, a tool that converts MathML notation to ready-to-compile code. See http://activemesa.com/mathsharp for more information.

231

We can then write a function that constructs a union case given a name and a set of parameters:

```
let makeCase parameters =
    try
      let caseInfo = cases.Item name
      (caseInfo parameters) :?> Expression
    with
    | exp -> raise <| new Exception(String.Format("Failed to
      create {0} : {1}", name, exp.Message))
```

In this listing, the variable name is captured implicitly, as the makeCase function is an inner function. Let's not jump ahead, though. We are interested in, of course, parsing and transforming some piece of XML. Here's how that process would begin:

```
use stringReader = new StringReader(text)
use xmlReader = XmlReader.Create(stringReader)
let doc = XDocument.Load(xmlReader)
let parsed = recursiveBuild doc.Root
```

So, what is this recursiveBuild function? As its name suggests, it is a function that recursively turns an XML element into a case of our discriminated union. Here is the full listing:

```
let rec recursiveBuild (root:XElement) =
  let name = root.Name.LocalName |> makeCamelCase

  let makeCase parameters =
    // as before

  let elems = root.Elements() |> Seq.toArray
  let values = elems |> Array.map(fun f -> recursiveBuild f)
  if elems.Length = 0 then
    let rootValue = root.Value.Trim()
    makeCase [| box rootValue |]
```

```
else
  try
    values |> Array.map box |> makeCase
  with
  | _ -> makeCase [| values |> Array.toList |]
```

Let's try to go slowly through what's going on here:

- Because our union cases are camel-cased and the XML file is lowercase, I convert the name of the XML element (which we call root) to camel case.

- We materialize the sequence of child elements of the current elements into an array.

- For each inner element, we call recursiveBuild recursively (surprise!).

- Now we check how many child elements the current element has. If it is zero, it could be just a <value> with text in it. If it's not, there are two possibilities:

  - The item takes a bunch of primitives that can all be boxed into parameters.

  - The item takes a bunch of expressions.

This constructs the expression tree. If we want to evaluate the numeric value of the expression, this is now simple thanks to pattern matching:

```
let rec eval expr =
  match expr with
  | Math m -> eval m.Head
  | Plus (lhs, rhs) -> eval lhs + eval rhs
  | Value v -> v |> int
```

Similarly, you could define a function for printing an expression:

```
let rec print expr =
  match expr with
  | Math m -> print m.Head
  | Plus (lhs, rhs) -> String.Format("({0}+{1})", print lhs,
    print rhs)
  | Value v -> v
```

Putting it all together, we can now print the expression in human-readable form and evaluate its result:

```
let parsed = recursiveBuild doc.Root
printf "%s = %d" (print parsed) (eval parsed)
// (2+3) = 5
```

Both of the functions are, of course, crude implementations of the Visitor design pattern without any traditional OOP trappings (although they are, of course, present behind the scenes). Here are some things to note:

- Our Value case is of string. If we wanted it to store an integer or a floating-point number, our parsing code would have to pry this information away using reflection.

- Instead of making top-level functions, we can give Expression its own methods and even properties. For example, we can give it a property called Val that evaluates its numeric value:

  ```
  type Expression =
    // union members here
      member self.Val =
        let rec eval expr =
  ```

CHAPTER 16   INTERPRETER

```
match expr with
| Math m -> eval(m.Head)
| Plus (lhs, rhs) -> eval lhs + eval rhs
| Value v -> v |> int
eval self
```

- Strictly speaking, discriminated unions violate the Open-Closed Principle because there is no way to augment them through inheritance. As a result, if you decide to support new cases, you'd have to modify the original union type.

To sum up, discriminated unions, pattern matching, and also list comprehensions (which we have not used in our demo, but you would typically use them in a scenario like this) all make the Interpreter and Visitor patterns easy to implement under the functional paradigm.

Summary

First of all, it needs to be said that, comparatively speaking, the Interpreter design pattern is somewhat uncommon. The challenges of building parsers are nowadays considered nonessential, which is why I see it being removed from computer science courses in many universities (my own included). Also, unless you plan to work in language design or, say, making tools for static code analysis, you are unlikely to find skills in building parsers in high demand.

That said, the challenge of interpretation is a whole separate field of computer science to which a single chapter of a design patterns book cannot reasonably do justice. If you are interested in the subject,

I recommend you check out frameworks such as Lex/Yacc, ANTLR, and many others that are specifically geared for lexer and parser construction. I can also recommend writing static analysis plug-ins for popular IDEs. That is a great way to get a feel for how real Abstract Syntax Trees[3] look, how they are traversed, and even modified.

---

[3]An Abstract Syntax Tree (AST) is nothing more than a tree-based representation of code that can be traversed and, in some cases, even modified.

CHAPTER 17

Iterator

An Iterator, put simply, is an object that is used to traverse some structure or other. Typically, the Iterator references the currently accessed element and has a method to move forward. A bidirectional Iterator also lets you lets you walk backward, and a random-access Iterator allows you to access an element at an arbitrary position.

In .NET, the thing that enables the Iterator pattern (the .NET framework uses the term *enumerator* instead) typically implements the IEnumerator<T> interface. It has the following members:

- Current refers to the element at the current position.

- MoveNext() lets you move on to the next element of the collection; it returns true if we succeeded and false otherwise.

- Reset() sets the enumerator to the initial position.

The enumerator is also disposable, but we don't care about that too much. The point is, any time you write

```
foreach (x in y)
  Console.WriteLine(x);
```

what you are really doing is the equivalent of

```
var enumerator = ((IEnumerable<Foo>)y).GetEnumerator();
while (enumerator.MoveNext())
```

© Dmitri Nesteruk 2019
D. Nesteruk, *Design Patterns in .NET*, https://doi.org/10.1007/978-1-4842-4366-4_17

```
{
  temp = enumerator.Current;
  Console.WriteLine(temp);
}
```

In other words, a class that implements IEnumerable<T> is required to have a method called GetEnumerator() that returns an IEnumerator<T>. You use that enumerator to traverse the object.

Needless to say, it is very rare for you to have to make your own IEnumerator. Typically, you can write code such as this:

```
IEnumerable<int> GetSomeNumbers()
{
  yield return 1;
  yield return 2;
  yield return 3;
}
```

The rest of the operations will be taken care of by the compiler. Alternatively, you can just use an existing collection class (array, List<T>, etc.) that already has all the plumbing you need.

Array-Backed Properties

Not all things are easy to iterate. For example, you cannot iterate all fields in a class unless you are using reflection. Sometimes you need to, though. Here, let me show you a scenario.

Suppose you're making a game with creatures in it. These creatures have various attributes, such as strength, agility, and intelligence. You could implement them as

```
public class Creature
{
  public int Strength { get; set; }
  public int Agility { get; set; }
  public int Intelligence { get; set; }
}
```

Now you also want to output some aggregate statistics about the creature. For example, you decide to calculate the sum of all the creature's abilities:

```
public double SumOfStats => Strength + Agility + Intelligence;
```

This code is impossible to automatically refactor if you add an additional Wisdom property (is that too much Dungeons & Dragons nerdiness for you?), but let me show you something even worse. If you want the average of all the abilities, you would write:

```
public double AverageStat => SumOfStats / 3.0;
```

That 3.0 is a bona fide *magic number*, completely unsafe if the structure of the code changes. Let me show you yet another example of ugliness. Suppose you decide to calculate the maximum ability value of a creature. You would need to write something like this:

```
public double MaxStat => Math.Max(
  Math.Max(Strength, Agility), Intelligence);
```

Well, you get the idea. This code is not robust and will break on any small change, so we're going to fix it, and the implementation is going to make use of *array-backed properties.*

The idea of array-backed properties is simple: all of the backing fields of related properties exist in one array:

```
private int [] stats = new int[3];
```

239

Each of the properties then projects its getter and setter into the array. To avoid using integral indexes you can introduce private constants:

```
private const int strength = 0;
public int Strength
{
  get => stats[strength];
  set => stats[strength] = value;
}
// same for other properties
```

Now, of course, calculating the sum, average, and maximum statistics is really easy because the underlying field is an array, and arrays are supported in LINQ:

```
public double AverageStat => stats.Average();
public double SumOfStats => stats.Sum();
public double MaxStat => stats.Max();
```

If you want to add an extra property, all you need to do is:

- Extend the array by one element.

- Create a property with getter and setter.

That's it! The statistics will still be calculated correctly. Furthermore, if you want, you can eschew all of those methods we made in favor of

```
public IEnumerable<int> Stats => stats;
```

and just let the client perform his or her own LINQ queries directly; for example, `creature.Stats.Average()`. Finally, if you want `stats` to be the enumerable collection—that is, letting people write `foreach (var stat in creature)`—you can simply implement IEnumerable (and perhaps an indexer, too):

```
public class Creature : IEnumerable<int>
{
  // as before

  public IEnumerator<int> GetEnumerator()
    => stats.AsEnumerable().GetEnumerator();

  IEnumerator IEnumerable.GetEnumerator()
    => GetEnumerator();

  public int this[int index]
  {
    get => stats[index];
    set => stats[index] = value;
  }
}
```

Let's Make an Iterator

To appreciate just how ugly Iterators can get if you do decide to make them directly, we are going to implement a classic Computer Science example: tree traversal. Let's begin by defining a single node of a binary tree:

```
public class Node<T>
{
  public T Value;
  public Node<T> Left, Right;
  public Node<T> Parent;

  public Node(T value)
  {
    Value = value;
  }
```

241

```
public Node(T value, Node<T> left, Node<T> right)
{
  Value = value;
  Left = left;
  Right = right;

  left.Parent = right.Parent = this;
}
}
```

I have thrown in an additional constructor that initializes its node with both left and right child nodes. This allows us to define chained constructor trees such as:

```
//    1
//   / \
//  2   3
var root = new Node<int>(1,
  new Node<int>(2), new Node<int>(3));
```

Now we want to traverse the tree. If you remember your Data Structures and Algorithms course, you'll know that there are three ways: in-order, preorder, and postorder. Suppose we decide to define an InOrderIterator. Here's what it would look like:

```
public class InOrderIterator<T>
{
  public Node<T> Current { get; set; }
  private readonly Node<T> root;
  private bool yieldedStart;
```

```
public InOrderIterator(Node<T> root)
{
  this.root = Current = root;
  while (Current.Left != null)
    Current = Current.Left;
}

public bool MoveNext()
{
  // todo
}
}
```

This is not bad so far: just as if we were implementing IEnumerator<T>, we have a property called Current and a MoveNext() method. Here's the thing: because the Iterator is stateful, every invocation of MoveNext() has to take us to the next element in our current traversal scheme. This isn't as easy as it sounds:

```
public bool MoveNext()
{
  if (!yieldedStart)
  {
    yieldedStart = true;
    return true;
  }

  if (Current.Right != null)
  {
    Current = Current.Right;
    while (Current.Left != null)
      Current = Current.Left;
    return true;
  }
```

```
  else
  {
    var p = Current.Parent;
    while (p != null && Current == p.Right)
    {
      Current = p;
      p = p.Parent;
    }
    Current = p;
    return Current != null;
  }
}
```

I bet you weren't expecting this! Well this is exactly what you get if you implement your own Iterators directly: an unreadable mess. But it works! We can use the Iterator directly, C++ style:

```
var it = new InOrderIterator<int>(root);
while (it.MoveNext())
{
  Write(it.Current.Value);
  Write(',');
}
WriteLine();
// prints 213
```

Or, if we want, we can construct a dedicated BinaryTree class that exposes this in-order Iterator as a default one:

```
public class BinaryTree<T>
{
  private Node<T> root;
```

```
public BinaryTree(Node<T> root)
{
  this.root = root;
}

public InOrderIterator<T> GetEnumerator()
{
  return new InOrderIterator<T>(root);
}
}
```

Notice we don't even have to implement IEnumerable (thanks to duck typing[1]). We can now write:

```
var root = new Node<int>(1,
  new Node<int>(2), new Node<int>(3));
var tree = new BinaryTree<int>(root);
foreach (var node in tree)
  WriteLine(node.Value); // 2 1 3
```

Improved Iteration

Our implementation of in-order iteration is virtually unreadable and is nothing like what you read in textbooks. Why? Lack of recursion. After all, MoveNext() cannot preserve its state, so every time it gets invoked, it starts from scratch without remembering its context: It only remembers the previous element, which needs to be found before we find the next one in the iteration scheme we are using.

---

[1]*Duck typing* is the idea that "if it walks like a duck and it quacks like a duck, it is a duck." In programming parlance, duck typing implies that the right code will be used even when it doesn't implement any particular interface to identify it. In our case, the foreach keyword doesn't care in the least whether your type implements IEnumerable or not—all it's looking for is the implementation of GetEnumerator() in the iterated class. If it finds it, everything works.

This is why yield return exists: You can construct a state machine behind the scenes. This means that if I wanted to create a more natural in-order implementation, I could simply write it as:

```
public IEnumerable<Node<T>> NaturalInOrder
{
  get
  {
    IEnumerable<Node<T>> TraverseInOrder(Node<T> current)
    {
      if (current.Left != null)
      {
        foreach (var left in TraverseInOrder(current.Left))
          yield return left;
      }
      yield return current;
      if (current.Right != null)
      {
        foreach (var right in TraverseInOrder(current.Right))
          yield return right;
      }
    }
    foreach (var node in TraverseInOrder(root))
      yield return node;
  }
}
```

Notice that all the calls here are recursive. Now what we can do is use this directly; for example:

```
var root = new Node<int>(1,
  new Node<int>(2), new Node<int>(3));
var tree = new BinaryTree<int>(root);
WriteLine(string.Join(",", tree.NaturalInOrder.Select(x =>
x.Value)));
// 2,1,3
```

This is far better. The algorithm itself is readable and, once again, we can take the property and just do LINQ on it, no problem.

Summary

The Iterator design pattern has been deliberately hidden in C# in favor of the simple IEnumerator/IEnumerable duopoly on which everything is built. Notice that these interfaces only support forward iteration—there is no MoveBack() in IEnumerator. The existence of yield allows you to very quickly return elements as a collection that can be consumed by someone else while being blissfully unaware of the state machine that gets built behind the scenes.

CHAPTER 18

Mediator

A large proportion of the code we write has different components (classes) communicating with one another through direct references. However, there are situations when you don't necessarily want objects to be aware of each other's presence. Or perhaps you do want them to be aware of one another, but you still don't want them to communicate through references, because as soon as you keep and hold a reference to something, you extend that object's lifetime beyond what might originally be desired (unless it is a WeakReference, of course).

The Mediator is a mechanism for facilitating communication between the components. Naturally, the mediator itself needs to be accessible to every component taking part, which means it should either be a publicly available static variable or, alternatively, just a reference that gets injected into every component.

Chat Room

Your typical Internet chat room is the classic example of the Mediator design pattern, so let's implement this before we move on to the more complicated material.

© Dmitri Nesteruk 2019

D. Nesteruk, *Design Patterns in .NET*, https://doi.org/10.1007/978-1-4842-4366-4_18

The most trivial implementation of a participant in a chat room can be as simple as this:

```csharp
public class Person
{
  public string Name;
  public ChatRoom Room;
  private List<string> chatLog = new List<string>();

  public Person(string name) => Name = name;

  public void Receive(string sender, string message)
  {
    string s = $"{sender}: '{message}'";
    WriteLine($"[{Name}'s chat session] {s}");
    chatLog.Add(s);
  }

  public void Say(string message) => Room.Broadcast(Name, message);

  public void PrivateMessage(string who, string message)
  {
    Room.Message(Name, who, message);
  }
}
```

So we have a person with a Name (user ID), a chat log, and a reference to the actual ChatRoom. We have a constructor and then three methods:

- Receive() allows us to receive a message. Typically what this function would do is show the message on the user's screen, and also add it to the chat log.

- Say() allows the person to broadcast a message to everyone in the room.

- PrivateMessage() is private messaging functionality.
  You need to specify the name of the person for whom
  the message is intended.

Both Say() and PrivateMessage()[1] just relay operations to the chat
room. Speaking of which, let's actually implement ChatRoom—it's not
particularly complicated.

```
public class ChatRoom
{
  private List<Person> people = new List<Person>();

  public void Broadcast(string source, string message) { ... }
  public void Join(Person p) { ... }
  public void Message(string source, string destination,
    string message) { ...  }
}
```

I have decided to go with pointers here. The ChatRoom API is very
simple:

- Join() gets a person to join the room. We are not going
  to implement Leave(), instead deferring the idea to a
  subsequent example in this chapter.

- Broadcast() sends the message to almost everyone:
  we don't need to send the message back to the person
  who sent it.

- Message() sends a private message.

---

[1] In the real world, I would probably call the method PM(), considering how
commonplace that acronym has become.

The implementation of Join() is as follows:

```
public void Join(Person p)
{
  string joinMsg = $"{p.Name} joins the chat";
  Broadcast("room", joinMsg);

  p.Room = this;
  people.Add(p);
}
```

Just like a classic Internet Relay Chat (IRC) chat room, we broadcast the message that someone has joined to everyone in the room. The first argument of Broadcast(), the origin parameter, in this case, is specified as "room" rather than the person who has joined. We then set the person's room reference and add that person to the list of people in the room.

Now, let's look at Broadcast(): this is where a message is sent to every room participant. Remember, each participant has its own Person. Receive() method for processing the message, so the implementation is somewhat trivial:

```
public void Broadcast(string source, string message)
{
  foreach (var p in people)
    if (p.Name != source)
      p.Receive(source, message);
}
```

Whether or not we want to prevent a broadcast message to be relayed to ourselves is a point of debate, but I am actively avoiding it here. Everyone else gets the message, though.

Finally, here is private messaging implemented with Message():

```
public void Message(string source, string destination, string
message)
{
  people.FirstOrDefault(p => p.Name == destination)
    ?.Receive(source, message);
}
```

This searches for the recipient in the list of people and, if the recipient is found (because who knows, he or she could have left the room), dispatches the message to that person.

Returning to Person's implementations of Say() and PrivateMessage(), here they are:

```
public void Say(string message) => Room.Broadcast(Name, message);
```

```
public void PrivateMessage(string who, string message)
{
  Room.Message(Name, who, message);
}
```

As for Receive(), well, this is a good place to actually display the message on-screen as well as add it to the chat log.

```
public void Receive(string sender, string message)
{
  string s = $"{sender}: '{message}'";
  WriteLine($"[{Name}'s chat session] {s}");
  chatLog.Add(s);
}
```

We go the extra mile here by displaying not just who the message came from, but whose chat session we are currently in—this will be useful for diagnosing who said what and when.

Here is the scenario that we'll run through:

```
var room = new ChatRoom();

var john = new Person("John");
var jane = new Person("Jane");

room.Join(john);
room.Join(jane);

john.Say("hi room");
jane.Say("oh, hey john");

var simon = new Person("Simon");
room.Join(simon);
simon.Say("hi everyone!");

jane.PrivateMessage("Simon", "glad you could join us!");
```

Here is the output:

```
[john's chat session] room: "jane joins the chat"
[jane's chat session] john: "hi room"
[john's chat session] jane: "oh, hey john"
[john's chat session] room: "simon joins the chat"
[jane's chat session] room: "simon joins the chat"
[john's chat session] simon: "hi everyone!"
[jane's chat session] simon: "hi everyone!"
[simon's chat session] jane: "glad you could join us, simon"
```

Mediator with Events

In the chat room example, we have encountered a consistent theme: The participants need notification whenever someone posts a message. This seems like a perfect scenario for the Observer pattern, which is discussed in Chapter 21: the idea of the mediator having an event that is shared by all participants; participants can then subscribe to the event to receive notifications, and they can also cause the event to fire, thus triggering said notifications.

Instead of redoing the chat room once again, let's go for a simpler example: Imagine a game of football (soccer for my readers in the United States) with players and a coach. When the coach sees his or her team scoring, that coach naturally wants to congratulate the player. Of course, the coach needs some information about the event, like who scored the goal and how many goals the team has scored so far.

We can introduce a base class for any sort of event data:

```
abstract class GameEventArgs : EventArgs
{
  public abstract void Print();
}
```

I have added the Print() deliberately to print the event's contents to the command line. Now, we can derive from this class to store some goal-related data:

```
class PlayerScoredEventArgs : GameEventArgs
{
  public string PlayerName;
  public int GoalsScoredSoFar;

  public PlayerScoredEventArgs
    (string playerName, int goalsScoredSoFar)
  {
    PlayerName = playerName;
    GoalsScoredSoFar = goalsScoredSoFar;
  }
```

```csharp
public override void Print()
{
  WriteLine($"{PlayerName} has scored!" +
            $"(their {GoalsScoredSoFar} goal)");
}
}
```

We are once again going to build a mediator, but it will have no behaviors! Seriously, with an event-driven infrastructure, they are no longer needed:

```csharp
class Game
{
  public event EventHandler<GameEventArgs> Events;

  public void Fire(GameEventArgs args)
  {
    Events?.Invoke(this, args);
  }
}
```

As you can see, we've just made a central place where all game events are being generated. The generation itself is polymorphic: The event uses a GameEventArgs type, and you can test the argument against the various types available in your application. The Fire() utility method just helps us safely raise the event.

We can now construct the Player class. A player has a name, the number of goals he or she scored during the match, and a reference to the mediator Game, of course:

```csharp
class Player
{
  private string name;
  private int goalsScored = 0;
  private Game game;
```

```
public Player(Game game, string name)
{
  this.name = name;
  this.game = game;
}

public void Score()
{
  goalsScored++;
  var args = new PlayerScoredEventArgs(name, goalsScored);
  game.Fire(args);
}
}
```

The Player.Score() method is where we make
PlayerScoredEventArgs and post them for all subscribers to see. Who gets
this event? Why, a Coach, of course:

```
class Coach
{
  private Game game;

  public Coach(Game game)
  {
    this.game = game;

    // celebrate if player has scored <3 goals
    game.Events += (sender, args) =>
    {
      if (args is PlayerScoredEventArgs scored
          && scored.GoalsScoredSoFar < 3)
```

```
    {
      WriteLine($"coach says: well done, {scored.PlayerName}");
    }
  };
  }
}
```

The implementation of the Coach class is trivial; our coach doesn't even get a name. We do give him a constructor where a subscription is created to a game's Events such that, whenever something happens, the coach gets to process the event data in the provided lambda.

Notice that the argument type of the lambda is GameEventArgs—we don't know if a player has scored or has been sent off, so we need a cast to determine we've got the right type.

The interesting thing is that all the magic happens at the setup stage: There's no need to explicitly subscribe to particular events. The client is free to create objects using his or her constructors and then, when the player scores, the notifications are sent:

```
var game = new Game();
var player = new Player(game, "Sam");
var coach = new Coach(game);

player.Score(); // coach says: well done, Sam
player.Score(); // coach says: well done, Sam
player.Score(); //
```

The output is only two lines long because, on the third goal, the coach isn't impressed anymore.

Summary

The Mediator design pattern is all about having an in-between component that everyone in a system has a reference to and can use to communicate with one another. Instead of direct references, communication can happen through identifiers (usernames, unique IDs, etc.).

The simplest implementation of a Mediator is a member list and a function that goes through the list and does what it is intended to do—whether on every element of the list, or selectively.

A more sophisticated implementation of Mediator can use events to allow participants to subscribe (and unsubscribe) to things happening in the system. This way, messages sent from one component to another can be treated as events. In this setup, it is also easy for participants to unsubscribe to certain events if they are no longer interested in them or if they are about to leave the system altogether.

CHAPTER 19

Memento

When we looked at the Command design pattern, we noted that recording a list of every single change theoretically allows you to roll back the system to any point in time—after all, you've kept a record of all the modifications.

Sometimes, though, you don't really care about playing back the state of the system, but you do care about being able to roll back the system to a particular state, if need be.

This is precisely what the Memento pattern does: It typically stores the state of the system and returns it as a dedicated, read-only object with no behavior of its own. This "token," if you will, can be used only for feeding it back into the system to restore it to the state it represents. Let's look at an example.

Bank Account

Let's use the example of a bank account that we have made before.

```
public class BankAccount
{
  private int balance;

  public BankAccount(int balance)
  {
    this.balance = balance;
  }
```

© Dmitri Nesteruk 2019
D. Nesteruk, *Design Patterns in .NET*, https://doi.org/10.1007/978-1-4842-4366-4_19

```
// todo: everything else :)
}
```

Now, though, we decide to make a bank account with a Deposit(). Instead of it being void as in previous examples, Deposit() will now be made to return a Memento:

```
public Memento Deposit(int amount)
{
  balance += amount;
  return new Memento(balance);
}
```

and the Memento will then be usable for rolling back the account to the previous state:

```
public void Restore(Memento m)
{
  balance = m.Balance;
}
```

As for the Memento itself, we can go for a trivial implementation:

```
public class Memento
{
  public int Balance { get; }

  public Memento(int balance)
  {
    Balance = balance;
  }
}
```

Notice that the Memento class is immutable. Imagine if you could, in fact, change the balance: You could roll back the account to a state it was never in! Here is how one would go about using such a setup:

```
var ba = new BankAccount(100);
var m1 = ba.Deposit(50);
var m2 = ba.Deposit(25);
WriteLine(ba); // 175

// restore to m1
ba.Restore(m1);
WriteLine(ba); // 150

// restore back to m2
ba.Restore(m2);
WriteLine(ba); // 175
```

This implementation is good enough, although there are some things missing. For example, you never get a Memento representing the opening balance because a constructor cannot return a value. You could add an out parameter, of course, but that's just too ugly.

Undo and Redo

What if you were to store every Memento generated by BankAccount? In this case, you'd have a situation similar to our implementation of the Command pattern, where undo and redo operations are a by-product of this recording. Let's see how we can get undo and redo functionality with a Memento.

We'll introduce a new `BankAccount` class that is going to keep hold of every single Memento it ever generates:

```
public class BankAccount
{
  private int balance;
  private List<Memento> changes = new List<Memento>();
  private int current;

  public BankAccount(int balance)
  {
    this.balance = balance;
    changes.Add(new Memento(balance));
  }
}
```

We have now solved the problem of returning to the initial balance: The Memento for the initial change is stored as well. Of course, this Memento isn't actually returned, so to roll back to it, I suppose you could implement some `Reset()` function or something—that is totally up to you.

The `BankAccount` class has a `current` member that stores the index of the latest Memento. Hold on, why do we need this? Isn't it the case that `current` will always be one less than the list of `changes`? Only if you want to support undo or rollback operations; if you want redo operations too, you need this!

Now, here is the implementation of the `Deposit()` method:

```
public Memento Deposit(int amount)
{
  balance += amount;
  var m = new Memento(balance);
  changes.Add(m);
  ++current;
  return m;
}
```

There are several things that happen here:

- The balance is increased by the amount you wanted to deposit.

- A new memento is constructed with the new balance and added to the list of changes.

- We increase the current value (you can think of it as a pointer into the list of changes).

Now here comes the fun stuff. We add a method to restore the account state based on a Memento:

```
public void Restore(Memento m)
{
  if (m != null)
  {
    balance = m.Balance;
    changes.Add(m);
    current = changes.Count - 1;
  }
}
```

The restoration process is significantly different than the one we looked at earlier. First, we actually check that the Memento is initialized. This is relevant because we now have a way of signaling no-ops: just return a default value. Also, when we restore a Memento, we actually add that Memento to the list of changes so an undo operation will work correctly on it.

Now, here is the (rather tricky) implementation of Undo():

```
public Memento Undo()
{
  if (current > 0)
```

```
  {
    var m = changes[--current];
    balance = m.Balance;
    return m;
  }
  return null;
}
```

We can only Undo() if current points to a change that is greater than zero. If that is the case, we move the pointer back, grab the change at that position, apply it, and then return that change. If we cannot roll back to a previous memento, we return null, which should explain why we check for null in Restore().

The implementation of Redo() is very similar:

```
public Memento Redo()
{
  if (current + 1 < changes.Count)
  {
    var m = changes[++current];
    balance = m.Balance;
    return m;
  }
  return null;
}
```

Again, we need to be able to redo something: If we can, we do it safely; if not, we do nothing and return null. Putting it all together, we can now start using the undo and redo functionality:

```
var ba = new BankAccount(100);
ba.Deposit(50);
ba.Deposit(25);
WriteLine(ba);
```

```
ba.Undo();
WriteLine($"Undo 1: {ba}"); // Undo 1: 150

ba.Undo();
WriteLine($"Undo 2: {ba}"); // Undo 2: 100

ba.Redo();
WriteLine($"Redo 2: {ba}"); // Redo 2: 150
```

Summary

The Memento pattern is all about handing out tokens that can be used to restore the system to a prior state. Typically, the token contains all the information necessary to move the system to a particular state, and, if it is small enough, you can also use it to record all the states of the system so as to allow not just the arbitrary resetting of the system to a prior state, but controlled navigation backward (undo) and forward (redo) of all the states the system was in.

One design decision that I made in the given demos is to make the Memento a class. This allows me to use the null value to encode the absence of a Memento to operate on. If we wanted to make it a struct instead, we would have to redesign the API so that, instead of null, the Restore() method would be able to take either a Nullable<Memento>, some Option<Memento> type (.NET doesn't have a built-in option type yet), or a Memento possessing some easily identifiable trait (e.g., a balance of int.MinValue).

CHAPTER 20

Null Object

We don't always choose the interfaces we work with. For example, I would rather have my car drive me to my destination by itself, without me having to give 100 percent of my attention to the road and the dangerous lunatics driving next to me. It's the same with software: sometimes you don't really want a piece of functionality, but it is built into the interface. So what do you do? You make a Null Object.

Scenario

Suppose you inherit a library that uses the following interface:

```
public interface ILog
{
  void Info(string msg);
  void Warn(string msg);
}
```

The library uses this interface to operate on bank accounts such as:

```
public class BankAccount
{
  private ILog log;
  private int balance;
```

© Dmitri Nesteruk 2019

D. Nesteruk, *Design Patterns in .NET*, https://doi.org/10.1007/978-1-4842-4366-4_20

```
public BankAccount(ILog log)
{
  this.log = log;
}

// more members here
}
```

In fact, BankAccount can have methods similar to:

```
public void Deposit(int amount)
{
  balance += amount;
  log.Info($"Deposited ${amount}, balance is now {balance}");
}
```

So, what's the problem here? Well, if you do need logging, there's no problem, you just implement your own logging class.

```
class ConsoleLog : ILog
{
  public void Info(string msg)
  {
    WriteLine(msg);
  }

  public void Warn(string msg)
  {
    WriteLine("WARNING:" + msg);
  }
}
```

You can then use it straight away. What if you don't want logging at all, though?

Intrusive Approach

The simplest approach, and one that breaks the OCP, is to change the interface to an abstract class; that is, change ILog to

```
public abstract class ILog
{
  void Info(string msg) {}
  void Warn(string msg) {}
}
```

You might want to follow up this change with a Rename refactoring from ILog to Log, but hopefully, the approach is obvious: By providing default no-op implementations in the base class, you can now simply make a dummy inheritor of this new ILog and supply it to whoever needs it. You can also go further, make it nonabstract, and then ILog is your Null Object insofar as no-op behavior is concerned.

This solution really assumes a lot, specifically that you are able to jump in and redesign your base class. If you have clients depending on ILog being an interface, you're in trouble.

Null Object

Look at BankAccount's constructor once again:

```
public BankAccount(ILog log)
{
  this.log = log;
}
```

Because the constructor takes a logger, it is *unsafe* to assume that you can get away with just passing it a null. BankAccount could be checking the pointer internally before dispatching on it, but you don't know that it does, and without extra documentation it is impossible to tell.

271

As a consequence, the only thing that would be reasonable to pass into BankAccount is a *Null Object*, a class that conforms to the interface but contains no functionality:

```
public sealed class NullLog : ILog
{
  public void Info(string msg) { }
  public void Warn(string msg) { }
}
```

Notice that the class is `sealed`: This is a design choice that presupposes that there is no point in inheriting from an object that deliberately has no behavior. Essentially, `NullLog` is a worthless parent.

Design Improvements

Stop and think for a moment: If `BankAccount` was under your control, could you improve the interface such that it is easier to use? Well, here are some ideas:

- Put reference checks everywhere. This sorts out the correctness on BankAccount's end, but doesn't stop getting library users confused. Remember, you're still not communicating that the reference can be `null`.

```
public void Deposit(int amount)
{
  balance += amount;
  log?.Info($"Deposited ${amount}, balance is now
  {balance}");
  // ^^ check for null here
}
```

- Add a default argument value, something like ILog
  log = null as a way of indicating that passing a null
  is generally okay. Notice that C# does not allow you to
  replace that null with something more meaningful,
  like a NoLogging that would refer to a private field.
  Even if you go for this approach, you would still have to
  perform checks on the pointer value in every location
  where you want to use the object, and that's a lot of
  null checks that are easy to miss!

- Use some optional type. This is idiomatically correct
  and communicates intent better than anything else.
  Why? Because it *forces* both the API writer and the
  API caller to tread carefully and perform appropriate
  checks. On the other hand, the caller can safely assume
  that passing in an Optional.None is a safe and expected
  operation.

Null Object Virtual Proxy

There is another radical idea that involves a double-hop around the ILog
bend. It involves subdividing the process of logging into invocation (we
want a nice ILog interface) and operation (what the logger actually does)
by operating through a proxy. Consider the following:

```
class OptionalLog: ILog
{
  private ILog impl;
  private static ILog NoLogging = null;

  public OptionalLog(ILog impl)
  {
    this.impl = impl;
  }
```

```
public void Info(string msg)
{
  impl?.Info(msg);
}
// and similar checks for other members
}
```

Now we have abstracted away invocation from implementation. What we do now is redefine the BankAccount constructor as follows:

```
public BankAccount(ILog log)
{
  this.log = new OptionalLog(log);
}
```

As you can see, there is clever subterfuge here: We are taking an ILog but storing an OptionalLog (this is the Virtual Proxy design pattern). Then, all the calls to this optional logger are safe; they only "happen" if the underlying object is available:

```
var account = new BankAccount(null);
account.Withdraw(int.MaxValue); // no crash
```

Dynamic Null Object

To construct a correct Null Object, you have to implement every member of the required interface. That is boring; can't we just write a single method that says, "Please just do nothing on any call?" It turns out that we can, thanks to the Dynamic Language Runtime (DLR).

For this example, we are going to make a type called Null<T> that will inherit from DynamicObject and simply provide a no-op response to any method that is called on it:

```
public class Null<T> : DynamicObject where T:class
{
  public override bool TryInvokeMember(InvokeMemberBinder
  binder, object[] args, out object result)
  {
    var name = binder.Name;
    result = Activator.CreateInstance(binder.ReturnType);
    return true;
  }
}
```

As you can see, all this dynamic object does is construct a default instance of whatever type the method in question actually returns. If our logger returned an int indicating the number of lines written to the log, our dynamic object would just return 0 (zero).

Now, I have neglected to mention what the T in Null<T> actually is. As you might have guessed, that's the interface for which we need a no-op object. We can create a utility property getter to actually construct instances of Null<T> that satisfy the interface T. For this, we are going to use the ImpromptuInterface library.[1]

```
public static T Instance
{
  get
```

---

[1]ImpromptuInterface is an open-source dynamic "duck casting" library built on top of DLR and Reflection.Emit. Its source code is available at https://github.com/ekonbenefits/impromptu-interface and you can install it directly from NuGet.

```
  {
    if (!typeof(T).IsInterface)
      throw new ArgumentException("I must be an interface type");

    return new Null<T>().ActLike<T>();
  }
}
```

In this code, the ActLike() method from ImpromptuInterface takes a dynamic object and conforms it at runtime to the required interface T.

Putting everything together, we can now write the following:

```
var log = Null<ILog>.Instance;
var ba = new BankAccount(log);
ba.Deposit(100);
ba.Withdraw(200);
```

Once again, this code has a computational cost related to the construction of a dynamic object that not only does no-ops, but also conforms to the chosen interface.

Summary

The Null Object pattern raises an issue of API design: What kinds of assumptions can we make about the objects we depend on? If we are taking a reference, do we then have an obligation to check this reference on every use?

If you feel no such obligation, then the only way the client can implement a Null Object is to contruct a no-op implementation of the required interface and pass that instance in. That said, this only works well with methods: If the object's fields are also being used, for example, then you are in real trouble. The same goes for nonvoid methods where the return values are actually used for something.

If you want to proactively support the idea of Null Objects being passed as arguments, you need to be explicit about it: Either specify the parameter type as some Optional, give the parameter a default value that hints at a possible null, or just write documentation that explains what kind of value is expected at this location.

CHAPTER 21

Observer

The Observer pattern, quite simply, lets one component notify other components that something has happened. The pattern is used all over the place; for example, when binding data to the UI, we can program domain objects such that, when they change, they generate notifications that the UI can subscribe to and update the visuals.

The Observer pattern is a popular and necessary pattern, so it is not surprising that the designers of C# decided to incorporate the pattern into the language wholesale with the use of the event keyword. The use of events in C# typically uses a convention that mandates the following:

- Events can be members of a class, and are decorated with the event keyword.

- Event handlers—methods that are called whenever an event is raised—are attached to the event with the += operator and are detached with the -= operator.

- An event handler typically takes two arguments:

  - An object reference to who exactly fired the event.

  - An object that (typically) derives from EventArgs that contains any necessary information about the event.

© Dmitri Nesteruk 2019

D. Nesteruk, *Design Patterns in .NET*, https://doi.org/10.1007/978-1-4842-4366-4_21

The exact *type* of an event that is used is typically a delegate. Just like the Action/Func wrappers for lambdas, the delegate wrappers for events are called EventHandler and exist in both nongeneric (that takes an EventArgs) and generic (that takes a type parameter that derives from EventArgs) second arguments. The first argument is always an object.

Here is a trivial example: suppose, whenever a person falls ill, we call a doctor. First, we define event arguments; in our case we just need the address to which to send the doctor:

```
public class FallsIllEventArgs : EventArgs
{
  public string Address;
}
```

Now, we can implement a Person type, which can look like this:

```
public class Person
{
  public void CatchACold()
  {
    FallsIll?.Invoke(this,
      new FallsIllEventArgs { Address = "123 London Road" });
  }

  public event EventHandler<FallsIllEventArgs> FallsIll;
}
```

As you can see, we are using a strongly typed EventHandler delegate to expose a public event. The CatchACold() method is used to raise the event, with the safe access ?. operator being used to ensure that, if the event doesn't have any subscribers, we don't get a NullReferenceException.

All that remains is to set up a scenario and provide an event handler:

```
static void Main()
{
  var person = new Person();
  person.FallsIll += CallDoctor;
  person.CatchACold();
}

private static void CallDoctor(object sender, FallsIllEventArgs
eventArgs)
{
  Console.WriteLine($"A doctor has been called to
  {eventArgs.Address}");
}
```

The event handler can be an ordinary (member) method, a local function, or a lambda; this is your choice. The signature is mandated by the original delegate; because we're using a strongly typed `EventHandler` variant, the second argument is `FallsIllEventArgs`. As soon as `CatchACold()` is called, the `CallDictor()` method is triggered.

Any given event can have more than one handler (C# delegates are multicast, after all). Removal of event handlers is typically done with the `-=` operator. When all subscribers have unsubscribed from an event, the event instance is set to `null`.

Weak Event Pattern

Did you know that .NET programs can have memory leaks? Not in the C++ sense, of course, but it is possible to keep holding on to an object for longer than necessary. Specifically, you can make an object and set its reference to `null` but it will still be alive. How? Let me show you.

First, let's make a Button class:

```
public class Button
{
  public event EventHandler Clicked;

  public void Fire()
  {
    Clicked?.Invoke(this, EventArgs.Empty);
  }
}
```

Now let's suppose we have this button in a window. For the sake of simplicity, I'll just stick it into a Window constructor:

```
public class Window
{
  public Window(Button button)
  {
    button.Clicked += ButtonOnClicked;
  }

  private void ButtonOnClicked(object sender,
  EventArgs eventArgs)
  {
    WriteLine("Button clicked (Window handler)");
  }

  ~Window()
  {
    WriteLine("Window finalized");
  }
}
```

This looks innocent enough, except it's not. If you make a button and a window, then set the window to null, it will still be alive! Here is the proof:

```
var btn = new Button();
var window = new Window(btn);
var windowRef = new WeakReference(window);
btn.Fire();

window = null;

FireGC();
WriteLine($"Is window alive after GC? {windowRef.IsAlive}");
// True
```

The window reference is still alive because it has a subscription to the button. When a button is clicked, the expectation is that something sensible happens: because there is a subscription to this event, the object that happens to have made this subscription cannot be allowed to be destroyed, even if the only reference to that object has been set to null. This is a memory leak in the .NET sense.

How can we fix this? One approach would be to use the WeakEventManager class from System.Windows. This class is specifically designed to allow the listener's handlers to be garbage-collected even if the source object persists. This class is very simple to use:

```
public class Window2
{
  public Window2(Button button)
  {
    WeakEventManager<Button, EventArgs>
      .AddHandler(button, "Clicked", ButtonOnClicked);
  }
  // rest of class same as before
}
```

Repeating the scenario again, this `Window2` implementation gives a `windowRef.IsAlive` result of `False`, as desired.

Property Observers

People get old; it's a fact of life. When someone gets older by a year, we might want to congratulate them on their birthday. But how? Given a definition such as this:

```
class Person
{
  public int Age { get; set; }
}
```

How do we know when a person's age changes? We don't. To see changes, we could try polling: reading a person's age every 100 milliseconds and comparing the new value with the previous. This approach will work, but it is tedious and does not scale. We need to be smarter about this.

We know that we want to be informed on every *write* to a person's age field. Well, the only way to catch this is to make a property with a backing field; that is:

```
class Person
{
  private int age;

  public int Age
  {
    get => age;
    set
    {
      // todo: something here
      age = value;
    }
```

```
  }
}
```

The setter for Age is where we can notify whoever cares that age has, in fact, changed. But how? Instead of hand-rolling some type, we can use an existing INotifyPropertyChanged interface specifically designed for this. This interface requires that you define the following event:

```
public event PropertyChangedEventHandler PropertyChanged;
```

If you use ReSharper or Rider, you are going to automatically get a piece of code for raising the event:

```
[NotifyPropertyChangedInvocator]
protected virtual void OnPropertyChanged
  ([CallerMemberName] string propertyName = null)
{
  PropertyChanged?.Invoke(this,
    new PropertyChangedEventArgs(propertyName));
}
```

The only piece of information that this event conveys is the name of the property that changed—neither the old nor the new value of the property is included in the event argument. The name is sent as a string and, to avoid the proliferation of string literals in code, the generated method uses the [CallerMemberName] attribute to tell the compiler to insert it automatically. Here is how one would use this:

```
public int Age
{
  get => age;
  set
```

```
  {
    if (value == age) return;
    age = value;
    OnPropertyChanged();
  }
}
```

The first line of the setter checks that the age did, in fact, change, because if it remains the same, there is (presumably) no point in notifying anyone. You need to be careful when working with reference types, however, because some of them might diverge in their implementation of == and Equals(), although those two should really evaluate to the same result.

Dependency Problems

In Microsoft Excel, you can have cells contain calculations using values of other cells. This is very convenient: whenever a particular cell's value changes, Excel recalculates every single cell (including cells on other worksheets) that this cell affected. Those cells then cause the recalculation of every cell dependent on them, and so it goes until the entire dependency graph is traversed, however long it takes. It's a beautiful process.

The problem with properties (and with the Observer pattern generally) is exactly the same: sometimes a part of a class not only generates notifications, but affects other parts of the class and then those members also generate their own event notifications. Unlike Excel, .NET doesn't have a built-in way of handling this, so such a situation can quickly turn into a real mess.

Let me illustrate. People age 16 or older (the age could be different in your country) can vote, so suppose we want to be notified of changes to a person's voting rights:

```
public bool CanVote => Age >= 16;
```

Apart from the slightly confusing use of the =>/>= operators, this shows a real problem: we want to call NotifyPropertyChanged on CanVote, too, but it has no setter! Clearly, this invocation has to happen in Age's setter, seeing how CanVote is directly dependent on Age. However, if you were to correctly implement this setter, you would end up with something that is really ugly and confusing:

```
public int Age
{
  get => age;
  set
  {
    if (value == age) return;

    var oldCanVote = CanVote;
    age = value;
    OnPropertyChanged();

    if (oldCanVote != CanVote)
      OnPropertyChanged(nameof(CanVote));
  }
}
```

What is going on here? Well, we want to make sure that CanVote really changed, so we cache its old value, modify Age, and then check whether CanVote has in fact changed and, if it did, then and only then we notify.

Clearly, this approach is unsustainable. What if Age affects not one, but ten different properties? What if CanVote depends on more than one property? How would we track those dependencies if we wanted to have refactoring-friendly code?

One approach would be to introduce a base class that takes care of all the notification support. Instead of just a list, we can now keep a Dictionary of property names and properties by which they are affected:

```csharp
class PropertyNotificationSupport : INotifyPropertyChanged
{
  private readonly Dictionary<string, HashSet<String>> affectedBy
    = new Dictionary<string, HashSet<string>>();

  public event PropertyChangedEventHandler PropertyChanged;
}
```

The implementation of OnPropertyChanged() can now be a lot more sophisticated. Not only do we notify on the property that is changing, but also all the properties it affects:

```csharp
[NotifyPropertyChangedInvocator]
protected virtual void OnPropertyChanged
  ([CallerMemberName] string propertyName = null)
{
  PropertyChanged?.Invoke(this,
    new PropertyChangedEventArgs(propertyName));

  foreach (var affector in affectedBy.Keys)
    if (affectedBy[affector].Contains(propertyName))
      OnPropertyChanged(propertyName);
}
```

So far, so good, but how do we encode the fact that, say, CanVote depends on Age? Do we really need to initialize some extra table? This seems like too much work.

288

One solution to this problem is expression trees. If we were to define the CanVote getter as an expression tree, we could traverse the tree and automatically discover all the properties it depends on then and there. This is a high-tech solution, for sure!

We'll start by giving our PropertyNotificationSupport base class a method called property() that takes the name of a property as well as an Expression<Func<T>> that calculates the value of the property when requested:

```
protected Func<T> property<T>(string name, Expression<Func<T>>
expr)
{
  Console.WriteLine($"Creating computed property for expression
  {expr}");

  var visitor = new MemberAccessVisitor(GetType());
  visitor.Visit(expr);

  if (visitor.PropertyNames.Any())
  {
    if (!affectedBy.ContainsKey(name))
      affectedBy.Add(name, new HashSet<string>());

    foreach (var propName in visitor.PropertyNames)
      if (propName != name)
        affectedBy[name].Add(propName);
  }

  return expr.Compile();
}
```

The goal of this method is that, in addition to actually compiling the expression into executable form, it uses a MemberAccessVisitor to traverse the expression tree, find the names of all properties that this property depends on, and add them to the affectedBy dictionary. The visitor itself (hey, it's the Visitor design pattern!) can be a private inner class similar to the following:

```
private class MemberAccessVisitor : ExpressionVisitor
{
  private readonly Type declaringType;
  public IList<string> PropertyNames = new List<string>();

  public MemberAccessVisitor(Type declaringType)
  {
    this.declaringType = declaringType;
  }

  public override Expression Visit(Expression expr)
  {
    if (expr != null && expr.NodeType == ExpressionType.
    MemberAccess)
    {
      var memberExpr = (MemberExpression)expr;
      if (memberExpr.Member.DeclaringType == declaringType)
      {
        PropertyNames.Add(memberExpr.Member.Name);
      }
    }

    return base.Visit(expr);
  }
}
```

The purpose of this visitor is to be able to traverse the expression, find all instances of member access (e.g., this.Age), extract the names of those properties, and put them into a public list that can then be consumed. That's it.

Armed with this implementation, we can once again modify our class Person to make use of the base class and to expose CanVote in a way that would automatically enlist it on notifications when Age changes:

```
class Person : PropertyNotificationSupport
{
  private int age;

  public int Age { /* as before */ }

  private readonly Func<bool> canVote;
  public bool CanVote => canVote();

  public Person()
  {
    canVote = property(nameof(CanVote), () => Age >= 16);
  }
}
```

As you can see, there are plenty of new things in this listing:

- The Person class now inherits from PropertyNotificationSupport.

- A private variable called canVote has been added to store the compiled Expression<Func<bool>> as a Func<bool>.

- The canVote variable gets initialized in the constructor; sadly, there is no way to perform this call in the initializer.

- A public property called CanVote now simply returns the result of that function's call.

This might seem like overengineering, but this approach solves the problem of dependent properties: If you define them as shown earlier, you will get the right notifications on read-only properties (or any properties with dependencies), and the performance implications are minimal. The only issue this solution doesn't handle is cycles in dependencies (e.g., if A depends on B but B depends on A, or some A→B→C→A dependency). I leave this as an exercise for the reader.

Event Streams

With all these discussions of Observer, you might be interested to learn that the latest .NET Framework comes with two interfaces: `IObserver<T>` and `IObservable<T>`. These interfaces, which were coincidental with the release of Reactive Extensions (Rx) , are meant primarily to deal with reactive streams. It is not my intention to discuss the entirety of Reactive Extensions, but these two interfaces are worth mentioning.

Let's start with `IObservable<T>`. This is an interface that is generally similar to the interface of a typical .NET event. The only difference is that, instead of using the += operator for subscription, this interface requires that you implement a method called `Subscribe()`. This method takes an `IObserver<T>` as its only parameter. Remember, this is an interface, and, unlike in the case of events or delegates, there is no prescribed storage mechanism. You are free to use anything you want.

There is some extra icing on the cake: The notion of unsubscription is explicitly supported in the interface. The `Subscribe()` method returns an `IDisposable` with the understanding that the return token (Memento pattern at work) has a `Dispose()` method that unsubscribes the observer from the observable.

The second piece of the puzzle is the `IObserver<T>` interface. It is designed to provide push-based notifications through three specific methods:

- OnNext(T) gets invoked whenever a new event occurs.

- OnCompleted() gets invoked when the source has no more data to give.

- OnError()gets invoked whenever the observer has experienced an error condition.

Once again, this is just an interface, and how you handle this is up to you. For example, you can completely ignore both OnCompleted() and OnError().

Given these two interfaces, the implementation our trivial doctor-patient example is suddenly a lot less trivial. First of all, we need to encapsulate the idea of an *event subscription*. This is required because we need a Memento that implements IDisposable through which unsubscription can happen.

```
private class Subscription : IDisposable
{
  private Person person;
  public IObserver<Event> Observer;

  public Subscription(Person person, IObserver<Event> observer)
  {
    this.person = person;
    Observer = observer;
  }

  public void Dispose()
  {
    person.subscriptions.Remove(this);
  }
}
```

This class is an inner class of Person, which is a good hint at the
growing complexity of any object that wants to support event streams.
Now, coming back to Person, we want it to implement the IObservable<T>
interface. But what is T? Unlike the conventional events, there are no
guidelines mandating that we inherit from EventArgs. Sure, we could
continue using that type,[1] or we could construct our own, completely
arbitrary, hierarchy:

```
public class Event
{
  // anything could be here
}

public class FallsIllEvent : Event
{
  public string Address;
}
```

Moving on, we now have a base class Event, so we can declare Person
to be a generator of such events. As a consequence, our Person type would
implement IObservable<Event> and would take an IObserver<Event> in
its Subscribe() method. Here is the entire Person class with the body of
the Subscription inner class omitted:

```
public class Person : IObservable<Event>
{
  private readonly HashSet<Subscription> subscriptions
    = new HashSet<Subscription>();
```

---

[1]By the way, System.EventArgs is an empty type. All it has is a default constructor
(empty) and a static member EventArgs.Empty that is a Singleton Null Object
(double pattern headshot!) that indicates the event arguments have no data.

```
public IDisposable Subscribe(IObserver<Event> observer)
{
  var subscription = new Subscription(this, observer);
  subscriptions.Add(subscription);
  return subscription;
}

public void CatchACold()
{
  foreach (var sub in subscriptions)
    sub.Observer.OnNext(new FallsIllEvent {Address = "123
    London Road"});
}

private class Subscription : IDisposable { ... }
}
```

I'm sure you'll agree that this is much more complicated than just publishing a single event for clients to subscribe to! There are advantages to this, though. For example, you can choose your own policy with respect to repeat subscriptions, situations when a subscriber is trying to subscribe to some event again. One thing worth noting is that HashSet<Subscription> is not a thread-safe container. This means that if you want Subscribe() and CatchACold() to be callable concurrently, you would need to either use a thread-safe collection, locking, or perhaps something even fancier, like an ImmutableList.

The problems do not end there. Remember, a subscriber has to implement an IObserver<Event> now. This means that, to support the scenario previously shown, we would have to write the following:

```
public class Demo : IObserver<Event>
{
  static void Main(string[] args)
```

```
  {
    new Demo();
  }

  public Demo()
  {
    var person = new Person();
    var sub = person.Subscribe(this);
  }

  public void OnNext(Event value)
  {
    if (value is FallsIllEvent args)
      WriteLine($"A doctor has been called to {args.Address}");
  }

  public void OnError(Exception error){}
  public void OnCompleted(){}
}
```

This is, once again, quite a mouthful. We could have simplified the subscription by using a special Observable.Subscribe() static method, but Observable (without the I) is part of Reactive Extensions, a separate library that you might or might not want to use.

This is how you can build an Observer pattern using .NET's own interfaces, without using the event keyword. The main advantage of this approach is that the stream of events that is generated by an IObservable can be directly fed into various Rx operators. For example, using System.Reactive, the entire demo program just shown can turn into a single statement:

```
person
  .OfType<FallsIllEvent>()
  .Subscribe(args =>
    WriteLine($"A doctor has been called to {args.Address}"));
```

Observable Collections

If you bind a List<T> to a list box in either WinForms or WPF, changing the list won't update the UI. Why not? Because List<T> does not support the Observer pattern, of course. Its individual members might, but the list as a whole has no explicit way of notifying that its contents have changed. Admittedly, you could just make a wrapper where methods such as Add() and Remove() generate notifications. However, both WinForms and WPF come with *observable collections,* classes BindingList<T> and ObservableCollection<T>, respectively.

Both of these types behave as a Collection<T>, but the operations generate additional notifications that can be used, for example, by UI components to update the presentation layer when the collections change. For example, ObservableCollection<T> implements the INotifyCollectionChanged interface, which, in turn, has a CollectionChanged event. This event will tell you what action has been applied to the collection and will give you a list of both old and new items, as well as information about old and new starting indexes. In other words, you get everything that you need to, say, redraw a list box correctly depending on the operation.

One important thing to note is that neither BindingList<T> nor ObservableCollection<T> are thread-safe. So if you plan to read and write these collections from multiple threads, you need to build a threading proxy (hey, Proxy pattern!). There are, in fact, two options here:

- Inherit from an observable collection and just put common collection operations such as Add() behind a lock.

- Inherit from a concurrent collection (e.g., a ConcurrentBag<T>) and add INotifyCollectionChanged functionality.

You can find implementations of both of these approaches on StackOverflow and elsewhere. I prefer the first option, as it is a lot simpler.

297

Declarative Subscriptions

So far, most of our discussions have centered on the idea of explicit, imperative subscription to events, whether via the usual .NET mechanisms, Reactive Extensions, or something else. However, that's not the only way event subscriptions can happen.

Declarative subscriptions can rely on attributes. For example, you can have an event publisher declared as:

```csharp
public class FootballPlayer
{
  [Publishes("score")]
  public event EventHandler PlayerScored;

  public string Name { get; set; }

  public void Score()
  {
    PlayerScored?.Invoke(this, new EventArgs());
  }
}
```

A corresponding subscriber is defined as

```csharp
public class FootballCoach
{
  [SubscribesTo("score")]
  public void PlayerScored(object sender, EventArgs args)
  {
    var p = sender as FootballPlayer;
    Console.WriteLine("Well done, {0}!", p.Name);
  }
}
```

With these attributes, you can make sure that, whenever either of the objects is constructed, it automatically subscribes to the events generated by the other object. Of course, the connection between the event source decorated with [Publishes] and the event *sink* (a fancy name for subscriber) decorated with [SuscribesTo] can only be made if there is some centralized way of constructing both objects.

The most obvious way is using an IoC container, and the exact implementation depends on the container you go for. For example, suppose you decide to use the Unity container: In this case, you would first of all define an extension such as the following:

```
public class BrokerExtension : UnityContainerExtension
{
  protected override void Initialize()
  {
    Context.Container.RegisterInstance(Broker,
      new ExternallyControlledLifetimeManager());
    Context.Strategies.AddNew<BrokerReflectionStrategy>(
      UnityBuildStage.PreCreation);
    Context.Strategies.Add(new BrokerWireupStrategy(Broker),
                        UnityBuildStage.Initialization);
  }

  public EventBroker Broker { get; } = new EventBroker();
}
```

What is important here is that we are using an event broker (a Mediator/Observer that we've seen countless times in the book) for managing event subscriptions. The container extension exposes two strategies (as per the Strategy pattern):

- BrokerReflectionStrategy goes through the types and finds their declarative events and subscriptions.

- `BrokerWireupStrategy` actually connects sinks and sources in the event broker.

Both of these strategies are quite complicated and make extensive use of IoC container internals. Suffice it to say that Reflection is used to ensure that sinks connect to sources; naturally, the events implemented are weak so that an observable can be safely garbage-collected even if there are subscribers to some of its events.

Declarative event subscriptions make sense when you need to build large-scale, event-driven systems. Their use only works together with an IoC container or some other centalized method of object construction (e.g., your own service locator) such that all the appropriate events are connected at creation. Notice that subscriptions are not cancelled when the objects are disposed.

Summary

Generally speaking, we could have avoided discussing the Observer pattern in C# because the pattern itself is baked right into the language. That said, I have demonstrated some of the practical uses of the Observer (property change notifications) as well as some of the issues related to that (dependent properties). Furthermore, we looked at the way in which the Observer pattern is supported for reactive streams.

Thread safety is one concern when it comes to Observer, whether we are talking about individual events or entire collections. It shows up because several Observers on one component form a list (or similar structure) and then the question immediately arises as to whether that list is thread-safe and what exactly happens when it is being modified and iterated on (for purposes of notification) at the same time.

CHAPTER 22

State

I must confess, my behavior is governed by my state. If I didn't get enough sleep, I am going to be a bit tired. If I had a drink, I wouldn't get behind the wheel. All of these are *states* and they govern my behavior: how I feel, what I can and cannot do.

I can, of course, transition from one state to another. I can go get a coffee, and this will take me from sleepy to alert (I hope). In this case, we can think of coffee as a *trigger* that causes a transition of yours truly from sleepy to alert. Let me clumsily illustrate it for you:[1]

```
        coffee
sleepy --------> alert
```

The State design pattern is a very simple idea: state controls behavior, and state can be changed. The only thing that the jury is out on is who triggers the change from one state to another.

There are two ways in which we can model states:

- States are actual classes with behaviors, and these behaviors cause the transition from this state to another. In other words, a state's members are the options in terms of where we can go from that state.

---

[1]I lied, twice. First, I don't drive a car; I prefer electric bikes. Not that it affects drinking in any way—it is still not allowed. Second, I don't drink coffee.

© Dmitri Nesteruk 2019
D. Nesteruk, *Design Patterns in .NET*, https://doi.org/10.1007/978-1-4842-4366-4_22

- States and transitions are just enumerations. We have a special component called a *state machine* that performs the actual transitions.

Both of these approaches are viable, but the second approach is really the most common. We'll take a look at both of them, but I must warn you that I'll gloss over the first one, as this is not how people typically do things.

State-Driven State Transitions

We begin with the most trivial example out there: a light switch that can only be in the on and off states. The reason why we are choosing such a simple domain is that I want to highlight the madness (there's no other word for it) that a classic implementation of State brings, and this example is simple enough to do so without generating pages of code listings.

We are going to build a model where any state is capable of switching to some other state: This reflects the "classic" implementation of the State design pattern (as per the GoF book). First, let's model the light switch. All it has is a state and some means of switching from one state to another:

```
public class Switch
{
  public State State = new OffState();
}
```

This all looks perfectly reasonable: we have a switch that is in some state (either on or off). We can now define the State, which in this particular case is going to be an actual class.

```
public abstract class State
{
  public virtual void On(Switch sw)
  {
    Console.WriteLine("Light is already on.");
  }
```

```
  public virtual void Off(Switch sw)
  {
    Console.WriteLine("Light is already off.");
  }
}
```

This implementation is far from intuitive, so much so that we need to discuss it slowly and carefully, because from the outset, nothing about the State class makes sense.

Although the State is abstract (meaning you cannot instantiate it), it has nonabstract members that allow the switching from one state to another. To a reasonable person, this makes no sense. Imagine the light switch: it is the switch that changes states. The state itself is not expected to change itself, and yet it appears this is exactly what it does.

Perhaps most bewildering, though, the default behavior of State. On()/Off() claims that we are already in this state! Note that these methods are virtual. This will come together, somewhat, as we implement the rest of the example.

We now implement the On and Off states:

```
public class OnState : State
{
  public OnState()
  {
    Console.WriteLine("Light turned on.");
  }
  public override void Off(Switch sw)
  {
    Console.WriteLine("Turning light off...");
    sw.State = new OffState();
  }
}
// similarly for OffState
```

The constructor of each state simply informs us that we have completed the transition, but the transition itself happens in OnState. Off() and OffState.On(). That is where the switching occurs.

We can now complete the Switch class by giving it methods to actually switch the light on and off:

```
public class Switch
{
  public State State = new OffState();
  public void On()  { State.On(this);  }
  public void Off() { State.Off(this); }
}
```

So, putting it all together, we can run the following scenario:

```
LightSwitch ls = new LightSwitch(); // Light turned off
ls.On();   // Switching light on...
           // Light turned on
ls.Off(); // Switching light off...
          // Light turned off
ls.Off(); // Light is already off
```

Here is an illustrated transition from OffState to OnState:

```
          LightSwitch.On() -> OffState.On()
OffState ----------------------------------> OnState
```

On the other hand, the transition from OnState to OnState uses the base State class, the one that tells you that you are already in that state:

```
         LightSwitch.On() -> State.On()
OnState ------------------------------> OnState
```

Let me be the first to say that the implementation presented here is *terrible*. Although it is a nice demonstration of OOP equilibristics, it is an unreadable, unintuitive mess that goes against everything we learn about both OOP generally and design patterns in particular, specifically:

- A state typically does not switch itself.

- A list of possible transitions should not appear all over the place; it's best to keep it in one place (SRP).

- There is no need to have actual classes modeling states unless they have class-specific behaviors; this example could be reduced to something much simpler.

Maybe we should be using enums to begin with?

Handmade State Machine

Let's try to define a state machine for a typical phone conversation. First of all, we describe the states of a phone:

```
public enum State
{
  OffHook,
  Connecting,
  Connected,
  OnHold
}
```

We can now also define transitions between states, also as an enum: fa

```
public enum Trigger
{
  CallDialed,
  HungUp,
```

```
  CallConnected,
  PlacedOnHold,
  TakenOffHold,
  LeftMessage
}
```

Now, the exact *rules* of this state machine (i.e., what transitions are possible) need to be stored somewhere. Let's use a dictionary of state-to-trigger/state pairs:

```
private static Dictionary<State, List<(Trigger, State)>> rules
  = new Dictionary<State, List<(Trigger, State)>>() { /* todo */ }
```

This is a little clumsy, but essentially the key of the dictionary is the State we're moving from, and the value is a list of Trigger-State pairs representing possible Triggers while in this State and the State you move into when you use the Trigger.

Let's initialize this data structure:

```
private static Dictionary<State, List<(Trigger, State)>> rules
  = new Dictionary<State, List<(Trigger, State)>>
  {
    [State.OffHook] = new List<(Trigger, State)>
    {
      (Trigger.CallDialed, State.Connecting)
    },
    [State.Connecting] = new List<(Trigger, State)>
    {
      (Trigger.HungUp, State.OffHook),
      (Trigger.CallConnected, State.Connected)
    },
    // more rules here
  };
```

We also need a starting (current) state, and we can also add an exit (terminal) state if we want the state machine to stop executing once that state is reached:

```
State state = State.OffHook, exitState = State.OnHook;
```

So in the preceding line, we start out with the OffHook state (when you're ready to make the call) and the exit state is when the phone is placed OnHook and the call is finished.

Having made this, we do not necessarily have to build a separate component for actually running (we use the term *orchestrating*) a state machine. For example, if we wanted to build an interactive model of the telephone, we could do it like this:

```
do
{
  Console.WriteLine($"The phone is currently {state}");
  Console.WriteLine("Select a trigger:");

  for (var i = 0; i < rules[state].Count; i++)
  {
    var (t, _) = rules[state][i];
    Console.WriteLine($"{i}. {t}");
  }

  int input = int.Parse(Console.ReadLine());

  var (_, s) = rules[state][input];
  state = s;
} while (state != exitState);
Console.WriteLine("We are done using the phone.");
```

The algorithm is fairly obvious: we let the user select one of the available triggers on the current state and, provided the trigger is valid, we transition to the right state by using the rules dictionary that we created earlier.

If the state we have reached is the exit state, we just jump out of the loop. Here's a sample interaction with the program:

```
The phone is currently OffHook
Select a trigger:
0. CallDialed
0
The phone is currently Connecting
Select a trigger:
0. HungUp
1. CallConnected
1
The phone is currently Connected
Select a trigger:
0. LeftMessage
1. HungUp
2. PlacedOnHold
2
The phone is currently OnHold
Select a trigger:
0. TakenOffHold
1. HungUp
1
We are done using the phone.
```

This hand-rolled state machine's main benefit is that it is very easy to understand: states and transitions are ordinary enumerations, the set of transitions is defined in a Dictionary, and the start and end states are simple variables. I am sure you'll agree this is much easier to understand than the example with which we started the chapter.

State Machines with Stateless

Hand-rolling a state machine works for the simplest of cases, but you probably want to leverage an industrial-strength state machine framework. That way, you get a tested library with a lot more functionality. It is also fitting because we need to discuss additional state machine-related concepts, and implementing them by hand is rather tedious.

Before we move on to the concepts I want to discuss, let us first reconstruct our previous phone call example using Stateless.[2] Assuming the existence of the same enumerations State and Trigger as before, the definition of a state machine is very simple:

```
var call = new StateMachine<State, Trigger>(State.OffHook);

phoneCall.Configure(State.OffHook)
  .Permit(Trigger.CallDialed, State.CallConnected);

// and so on, then, to cause a transition, we do

call.Fire(Trigger.CallDialed); // call.State is now State.
CallConnected
```

As you can see, Stateless's StateMachine class is a builder with a fluent interface. The motivation behind this API design will become apparent as we discuss the different intricacies of Stateless.

Types, Actions, and Ignoring Transitions

Let's talk about the many features of Stateless and state machines generally.

---

[2]Stateless can be found at `https://github.com/dotnet-state-machine/stateless`. It's worth noting that the phone call example actually comes from the authors of SimpleStateMachine, a project on which Stateless is based.

First and foremost, Stateless supports states and triggers of any .NET type—it is not constrained to enums. You can use strings, numbers, or anything else you want. For example, a light switch could use a bool for states (false = off, true = on); we'll keep using enums for triggers. Here is how one would implement the LightSwitch example:

```
// enum Trigger { On, Off }
var light = new StateMachine<bool, Trigger>(false);

light.Configure(false)            // if the light is off...
  .Permit(Trigger.On, true)       // we can turn it on
  .Ignore(Trigger.Off);           // but if it's already off we
                                  //    do nothing

// same for when the light is on
light.Configure(true)
  .Permit(Trigger.Off, false)
  .Ignore(Trigger.On)
  .OnEntry(() => timer.Start())
  .OnExit(() => timer.Stop());  // calculate time spent in this state

light.Fire(Trigger.On);   // Turning light on
light.Fire(Trigger.Off);  // Turning light off
light.Fire(Trigger.Off);  // Light is already off!
```

There are a few interesting things worth discussing here. First of all, this state machine has *actions,* things that happen as we enter a particular state. These are defined in OnEntry(), where you can provide a lambda that does something; similarly, you could invoke something at the moment the state is exited using OnExit(). One use of such transition actions would be to start a timer when entering a transition and stop it when exiting one, which could be used for tracking the amount of time spent in each state. For example, you might want to measure the time the light stays on for purposes of verifying electricity costs.

Another thing worth noting is the use of `Ignore()` builder methods. This basically tells the state machine to ignore the transition completely: If the light is already off, and we try to switch it off (as in the last line of the preceding code listing), we instruct the state machine to simply ignore it, so no output is produced in that case.

Why is this important? Because, if you forget to `Ignore()` this transition or fail to specify it explicitly, Stateless will throw an `InvalidOperationException`:

'No valid leaving transitions are permitted from state 'False' for trigger 'False'. Consider ignoring the trigger.'

Reentrancy Again

Another alternative to the redundant switching conundrum is Stateless's support for reentrant states. To replicate the example at the start of this chapter, we can configure the state machine so that, in the case of reentry into a state (meaning that we transition, say, from false to false), an action is invoked. Here is how one would configure it:

```
var light = new StateMachine<bool, Trigger>(false);

light.Configure(false) // if the light is off...
  .Permit(Trigger.On, true)  // we can turn it on
  .OnEntry(transition =>
  {
    if (transition.IsReentry)
      WriteLine("Light is already off!");
    else
      WriteLine("Turning light off");
  })
  .PermitReentry(Trigger.Off);

// same for when the light is on
```

311

```
light.Fire(Trigger.On);  // Turning light on
light.Fire(Trigger.Off); // Turning light off
light.Fire(Trigger.Off); // Light is already off!
```

In this listing, PermitReentry() allows us to return to the false (off) state on a Trigger.Off trigger. Notice that, to output a corresponding message to the console, we use a different lambda, one that has a Transition parameter. The parameter has public members that describe the transition fully. This includes Source (the state we are transitioning from), Destination (the state we are going to), Trigger (what caused the transition), and IsReentry, a Boolean flag that we use to determine if this is a reentrant transition.

Hierarchical States

In the context of a phone call, it can be argued that the OnHold state is a substate of the Connected state, implying that when we are on hold, we are also connected. Stateless lets us configure the state machine like this:

```
phoneCall.Configure(State.OnHold)
    .SubstateOf(State.Connected)
    // etc.
```

Now, if we are in the OnHold state, phoneCall.State will give us OnHold, but there is also a phoneCall.IsInState(State) method that will return true when called with either State.Connected or State.OnHold.

More Features

Let's talk about a few more features related to state machines that are implemented in Stateless.

- *Guard clauses* allow you to enable and disable transitions at will by calling PermitIf() and providing bool-returning lambda functions; for example:

```
phoneCall.Configure(State.OffHook)
  .PermitIf(Trigger.CallDialled, State.Connecting,
  () => IsValidNumber)
  .PermitIf(Trigger.CallDialled, State.Beeping,
  () => !IsValidNumber);
```

- *Parameterized triggers* are an interesting concept.
  Essentially, you can attach parameters to triggers
  such that, in addition to the trigger itself, there is also
  additional information that can be passed along. For
  example, if a state machine needs to notify a particular
  employee, you can specify an e-mail to be used for
  notification:

```
var notifyTrigger = workflow.SetTriggerParameters<string>
(Trigger.Notify);
workflow.Configure(State.Notified)
  .OnEntryFrom(assignTrigger, email => SendEmail(email));
workflow.Fire(notifyTrigger, "foo@bar.com");
```

- *External storage* is a feature of Stateless that lets you
  store the internal state of a state machine externally
  (e.g., in a database) instead of using the StateMachine
  class itself. To use it, you simply define the getter and
  setter methods in the StateMachine constructor:

```
var stateMachine = new StateMachine<State, Trigger>(
  () => database.ReadState(),
  s => database.WriteState(s));
```

- *Introspection* allows us to actually look at the table of
  triggers that can be fired from the current state through
  the PermittedTriggers property.

This is far from an exhaustive list of features that Stateless offers, but it covers all the important parts.

Summary

As you can see, the whole business of state machines extends way beyond simple transitions: It allows a lot of complexity to handle the most demanding business cases. Let us recap some of the state machine features we've discussed.

- State machines involve two collections: states and triggers. States model the possible states of the system and triggers transition us from one state to another. You are not limited to enumerations; you can use ordinary data types.

- Attempting a transition that is not configured will result in an exception.

- It is possible to explicitly configure entry and exit actions for each state.

- Reentrancy can be explicitly allowed in the API and, furthermore, you can determine whether or not a reentry is occuring in the entry or exit action.

- Transitions can be turned on and off through guard conditions. They can also be parameterized.

- States can be hierarchical; that is, they can be substates of other states. An additional method is then required to determine whether you're in a particular (parent) state.

Although most of this might seem like overengineering, these features provide great flexibility in defining real-world state machines.

CHAPTER 23

Strategy

Suppose you decide to take an array or vector of several strings and output them as a list:

- just
- like
- this

If you think about the different output formats, you probably know that you need to take each element and output it with some additional markup. In the case of languages such as HTML or LaTeX, though, the list will also need start and end tags or markers.

We can formulate a strategy for rendering a list:

- Render the opening tag or element.
- For each of the list items, render that item.
- Render the closing tag or element.

Different strategies can be formulated for different output formats, and these strategies can then be fed into a general, nonchanging algorithm to generate the text.

This is yet another pattern that exists in dynamic (runtime-replaceable) and static (generics-based, fixed) incarnations. Let's take a look at both of them.

© Dmitri Nesteruk 2019
D. Nesteruk, *Design Patterns in .NET*, https://doi.org/10.1007/978-1-4842-4366-4_23

Dynamic Strategy

Our goal is to print a simple list of text items in the following formats:

```
public enum OutputFormat
{
  Markdown,
  Html
}
```

The skeleton of our strategy will be defined in the following base class:

```
public interface IListStrategy
{
  void Start(StringBuilder sb);
  void AddListItem(StringBuilder sb, string item);
  void End(StringBuilder sb);
}
```

Now let us jump to our text processing component. This component would have a list-specific method called, say, AppendList().

```
public class TextProcessor
{
  private StringBuilder sb = new StringBuilder();
  private IListStrategy listStrategy;

  public void AppendList(IEnumerable<string> items)
  {
    listStrategy.Start(sb);
    foreach (var item in items)
      listStrategy.AddListItem(sb, item);
    listStrategy.End(sb);
  }

  public override string ToString() => sb.ToString();
}
```

So we've got a buffer called sb where all the output goes, the listStrategy that we are using for rendering lists, and of course AppendList(), which specifies the set of steps that need to be taken to actually render a list with a given strategy.

Now, pay attention here. Composition, as used earlier, is one of two possible options that can be taken to allow concrete implementations of a skeleton algorithm. Instead, we could add functions such as AddListItem() as abstract or virtual members to be overridden by derived classes; that's what the Template Method pattern does.

To return to our discussion, we can now go ahead and implement different strategies for lists, such as an HtmlListStrategy:

```
public class HtmlListStrategy : IListStrategy
{
  public void Start(StringBuilder sb) => sb.AppendLine("<ul>");
  public void End(StringBuilder sb) => sb.AppendLine("</ul>");

  public void AddListItem(StringBuilder sb, string item)
  {
    sb.AppendLine($"  <li>{item}</li>");
  }
}
```

By implementing the overrides, we fill in the gaps that specify how to process lists. We implement a MarkdownListStrategy in a similar fashion, but because Markdown does not need opening and closing tags, we only do work in the AddListItem() method:

```
public class MarkdownListStrategy : IListStrategy
{
  // markdown doesn't require list start/end tags
  public void Start(StringBuilder sb) {}
  public void End(StringBuilder sb) {}
```

```
public void AddListItem(StringBuilder sb, string item)
{
  sb.AppendLine($" * {item}");
}
}
```

We can now start using the TextProcessor, feeding it different strategies and getting different results. For example:

```
var tp = new TextProcessor();
tp.SetOutputFormat(OutputFormat.Markdown);
tp.AppendList(new []{"foo", "bar", "baz"});
WriteLine(tp);

// Output:
// * foo
// * bar
// * baz
```

We can make provisions for strategies to be switchable at runtime; this is precisely why we call this implementation a *dynamic* strategy. This is done in the SetOutputFormat() method, whose implementation is trivial:

```
public void SetOutputFormat(OutputFormat format)
{
  switch (format) {
    case OutputFormat.Markdown:
      listStrategy = new MarkdownListStrategy();
      break;
    case OutputFormat.Html:
      listStrategy = new HtmlListStrategy();
      break;
    default:
```

```
throw new ArgumentOutOfRangeException(nameof(format),
format, null);
}
}
```

Now, switching from one strategy to another is trivial, and you get to see the results straight away:

```
tp.Clear(); // erases underlying buffer
tp.SetOutputFormat(OutputFormat.Html);
tp.AppendList(new[] { "foo", "bar", "baz" });
WriteLine(tp);
```

```
// Output:
// <ul>
//   <li>foo</li>
//   <li>bar</li>
//   <li>baz</li>
// </ul>
```

Static Strategy

Thanks to the magic of generics, you can bake any strategy right into the type. Only minimal changes are necessary to the TextStrategy class:

```
public class TextProcessor<LS>
  where LS : IListStrategy, new()
{
  private StringBuilder sb = new StringBuilder();
  private IListStrategy listStrategy = new LS();
```

```
  public void AppendList(IEnumerable<string> items)
  {
    listStrategy.Start(sb);
    foreach (var item in items)
      listStrategy.AddListItem(sb, item);
    listStrategy.End(sb);
  }

  public override string ToString() => return sb.ToString();
}
```

What changed in the dynamic implementation is as follows: we added the LS generic argument, made a listStrategy member with this type, and started using it instead of the reference we had previously. The results of calling the adjusted AppendList() are identical to what we had before.

```
var tp = new TextProcessor<MarkdownListStrategy>();
tp.AppendList(new []{"foo", "bar", "baz"});
WriteLine(tp);

var tp2 = new TextProcessor<HtmlListStrategy>();
tp2.AppendList(new[] { "foo", "bar", "baz" });
WriteLine(tp2);
```

The output from this example is the same as for the dynamic strategy. Note that we have had to make two instances of TextProcessor, each with a distinct list-handling strategy, because it is impossible to switch a type's strategy midstream: it is baked right into the type.

Functional Strategy

The functional variation of the Strategy pattern is simple: All OOP constructs are simply replaced by functions. First of all, TextProcessor devolves from being a class to being a function. This is actually idiomatic (i.e., the right thing to do) because TextProcessor has a single operation.

```
let processList items startToken itemAction endToken =
  let mid = items |> (Seq.map itemAction) |> (String.concat "\n")
  [startToken; mid; endToken] |> String.concat "\n"
```

This function takes four arguments: a sequence of items, the starting token (note that it's a token, not a function), a function for processing each element, and the ending token. Because this is a function, this approach assumes that processList is stateless; that is, it does not keep any state internally.

As you can see from this, our strategy is not just a single, neatly self-contained element, but rather a combination of three different items: the start and end tokens as well as a function that operates on each of the elements in the sequence. We can now specialize processList to implement HTML and Markdown processing as before:

```
let processListHtml items =
  processList items "<ul>" (fun i -> "<li>" + i + "</li>") "</ul>"

let processListMarkdown items =
  processList items "" (fun i -> " * " + i) ""
```

This is how you would use these specializations, with predictable results:

```
let items = ["hello"; "world"]
printfn "%s" (processListHtml items)
printfn "%s" (processListMarkdown items)
```

The interesting thing to note about this example is that the interface of `processList` gives absolutely no hints whatsoever as to what the client is supposed to provide as the `itemAction`. All they know is that it is an `'a ->` `string`, so we rely on them to guess correctly what it is actually for.

Summary

The Strategy design pattern allows you to define a skeleton of an algorithm and then use composition to supply the missing implementation details related to a particular strategy. This approach exists in two incarnations:

- *Dynamic strategy* simply keeps a reference to the strategy currently being used. If you want to change to a different strategy, just change the reference.

- *Static strategy* requires that you choose the strategy at compile time and stick with it; there is no scope for changing your mind later on.

Should one use dynamic or static strategies? Well, dynamic strategies allow reconfiguration of the objects after they have been constructed. Imagine a UI setting that controls the form of the textual output: what would you rather have, a switchable `TextProcessor` or two variables of type `Text Processor<MarkdownStrategy>` and `TextProcessor<HtmlStrategy>`? It is really up to you.

CHAPTER 24

Template Method

The Strategy and Template Method design patterns are very similar, so much so that, just like with Factories, I would be very tempted to merge those patterns into a single Skeleton Method design pattern. I will resist the urge.

The difference between Strategy and Template Method is that Strategy uses composition (whether static or dynamic), whereas Template Method uses inheritance. The core principle of defining the skeleton of an algorithm in one place and its implementation details in other places remains, once again observing OCP (we simply extend systems).

Game Simulation

Most board games are very similar: The game starts (some sort of setup takes place), players take turns until a winner is decided, and then the winner can be announced. It doesn't matter what the game is—chess, checkers, something else—we can define the algorithm as follows:

```csharp
public abstract class Game
{
  public void Run()
  {
    Start();
    while (!HaveWinner)
      TakeTurn();
```

© Dmitri Nesteruk 2019
D. Nesteruk, *Design Patterns in .NET*, https://doi.org/10.1007/978-1-4842-4366-4_24

```
  WriteLine($"Player {WinningPlayer} wins.");
  }
}
```

As you can see, the `run()` method, which runs the game, simply uses a set of other methods and properties. Those methods are abstract, and also have protected visibility so they don't get called from the outside:

```
protected abstract void Start();
protected abstract bool HaveWinner { get; }
protected abstract void TakeTurn();
protected abstract int WinningPlayer { get; }
```

To be fair, some of these members, especially void-returning ones, do not necessarily have to be abstract. For example, if some games have no explicit start() procedure, having start() as abstract violates ISP because members that do not need it would still have to implement it. In the last chapter we deliberately made an interface, but with Template Method, the case is not as clear-cut.

Now, in addition to the preceding, we can have certain protected fields that are relevant to all games, the number of players and the index of the current player:

```
public abstract class Game
{
  public Game(int numberOfPlayers)
  {
    this.numberOfPlayers = numberOfPlayers;
  }

  protected int currentPlayer;
  protected readonly int numberOfPlayers;
  // other members omitted
}
```

From here on out, the Game class can be extended to implement a game of chess:

```
public class Chess : Game
{
  public Chess() : base(2) { /* 2 players */ }

  protected override void Start()
  {
    WriteLine($"Starting a game of chess with {numberOfPlayers}
    players.");
  }

  protected override bool HaveWinner => turn == maxTurns;

  protected override void TakeTurn()
  {
    WriteLine($"Turn {turn++} taken by player {currentPlayer}.");
    currentPlayer = (currentPlayer + 1) % numberOfPlayers;
  }

  protected override int WinningPlayer => currentPlayer;

  private int maxTurns = 10;
  private int turn = 1;
}
```

A game of chess involves two players, so that is the value fed into the base class's constructor. We then proceed to override all the necessary methods, implementing some very simple simulation logic for ending the game after ten turns. We can now use the class with new Chess().Run(); here is the output:

```
Starting a game of chess with 2 players
Turn 0 taken by player 0
Turn 1 taken by player 1
```

...
Turn 8 taken by player 0
Turn 9 taken by player 1
Player 0 wins.

That's pretty much all there is to it!

Functional Template Method

As you might have guessed, the functional approach to Template Method is to simply define a stand-alone function runGame() that takes the templated parts as parameters. The only problem is that a game is an inherently mutable scenario, which means we have to have some sort of container representing the state of the game. We can try using a record type:

```
type GameState = {
  CurrentPlayer: int;
  NumberOfPlayers: int;
  HaveWinner: bool;
  WinningPlayer: int;
}
```

With this setup, we end up having to pass an instance of GameState into every function that is part of the template method. The method itself, mind you, is rather simple:

```
let runGame initialState startAction takeTurnAction
haveWinnerAction =
  let state = initialState
  startAction state
  while not (haveWinnerAction state) do
    takeTurnAction state
  printfn "Player %i wins." state.WinningPlayer
```

The implementation of a chess game is not a particularly difficult affair either, the only real problem being the initialization and modification of internal state:

```
let chess() =
  let mutable turn = 0
  let mutable maxTurns = 10
  let state = {
    NumberOfPlayers = 2;
    CurrentPlayer = 0;
    WinningPlayer = -1;
  }
  let start state =
    printfn "Starting a game of chess with %i players" state.
    NumberOfPlayers

  let takeTurn state =
    printfn "Turn %i taken by player %i." turn state.CurrentPlayer
    state.CurrentPlayer <- (state.CurrentPlayer+1) % state.
    NumberOfPlayers
    turn <- turn + 1
    state.WinningPlayer <- state.CurrentPlayer

  let haveWinner state =
    turn = maxTurns

  runGame state start takeTurn haveWinner
```

Just to recap, what we are doing here is initializing all the functions required by the method or function right inside the outer function (this is completely legitimate in both C# and F#) and then pass each of those functions into runGame. Notice also that we have some mutable state that is used throughout the subfunction calls.

Overall, implementation of Template Method using functions instead of objects is quite possible if you are prepared to introduce record types and mutability into your code. Theoretically, you could rewrite this example and get rid of the mutable state by essentially storing a snapshot of each game state and passing that in a recursive setting. This would effectively turn a Template Method into a kind of templated State pattern. Try it!

Summary

Unlike the Strategy, which uses composition and thus branches into static and dynamic variations, Template Method uses inheritance and, as a consequence, it can only be static, as there is no way to manipulate the inheritance characteristics of an object once it has been constructed.

The only design decision in a Template Method is whether you want the methods used by the Template Method to be abstract or actually have a body, even if that body is empty. If you foresee some methods that are unnecessary for all inheritors, go ahead and make them empty or nonabstract so as to comply with ISP.

CHAPTER 25

Visitor

To explain this pattern I'm going to jump into an example first and then discuss the pattern itself. Suppose you have parsed a mathematical expression (with the use of the Interpreter pattern, of course) composed of double values and addition operators; for example,

```
(1.0 + (2.0 + 3.0))
```

This can expressed using an object hierarchy similar to the following:

```
public abstract class Expression { /* nothing here (yet) */ }

public class DoubleExpression : Expression
{
  private double value;

  public DoubleExpression(double value) { this.value = value; }
}

public class AdditionExpression : Expression
{
  private Expression left, right;

  public AdditionExpression(Expression left, Expression right)
  {
    this.left = left;
    this.right = right;
  }
}
```

© Dmitri Nesteruk 2019

D. Nesteruk, *Design Patterns in .NET*, https://doi.org/10.1007/978-1-4842-4366-4_25

Given this setup, you are interested in two things:

- Printing the OOP expression as text.

- Evaluating the expression's value.

You also want to do those two things (and many other possible operations on these trees) as uniformly and succintly as possible. How would you do it? Well, there are many ways and we'll take a look at them all, starting with the implementation of the printing operation.

Intrusive Visitor

The simplest solution is to take the base `Expression` class and add an abstract member to it.

```
public abstract class Expression
{
  // adding a new operation
  public abstract void Print(StringBuilder sb);
}
```

In addition to breaking OCP, this modification hinges on the assumption that you actually have access to the hierarchy's source code—something that is not always guaranteed. But we have to start somewhere, right? With this change, we need to implement `Print()` in `DoubleExpression` (that's easy, so I omit it here) as well as in `AdditionExpression`:

```
public class AdditionExpression : Expression
{
  ...
```

```
public override void Print(StringBuilder sb)
{
  sb.Append(value: "(");
  left.Print(sb);
  sb.Append(value: "+");
  right.Print(sb);
  sb.Append(value: ")");
}
}
```

This is fun! We are polymorphically and recursively calling Print() on subexpressions. Let's test this out:

```
var e = new AdditionExpression(
  left: new DoubleExpression(1),
  right: new AdditionExpression(
    left: new DoubleExpression(2),
    right: new DoubleExpression(3)));
var sb = new StringBuilder();
e.Print(sb);
WriteLine(sb); // (1.0 + (2.0 + 3.0))
```

This was easy, but now imagine you have ten inheritors in the hierarchy (not uncommon, by the way, in real-world scenarios) and you need to add some new Eval() operation. That's ten modifications that need to be done in ten different classes, but OCP isn't the real problem.

The real problem is SRP. You see, a problem such as printing is a special concern. Rather than stating that every expression should print itself, why not introduce an ExpressionPrinter that knows how to print expressions? Later on, you can introduce an ExpressionEvaluator that knows how to perform the actual calculations, all without affecting the Expression hierarchy in any way.

Reflective Printer

Now that we've decided to make a *separate* printer component, let's get rid of Print() member functions (but keep the base class, of course).

```
abstract class Expression
{
  // nothing here!
};
```

Now let's try to implement an ExpressionPrinter. My first instinct would be to write something like this:

```
public static class ExpressionPrinter
{
  public static void Print(DoubleExpression e, StringBuilder sb)
  {
    sb.Append(de.Value);
  }

  public static void Print(AdditionExpression ae, StringBuilder sb)
  {
    sb.Append("(");
    Print(ae.Left, sb);  // will not compile!!!
    sb.Append("+");
    Print(ae.Right, sb); // will not compile!!!
    sb.Append(")");
  }
}
```

Odds of that compiling are zero. C# knows that, say, ae.Left is an Expression, but because it doesn't check the type at runtime (unlike various dynamically typed languages), it doesn't know which overload to call. Too bad!

What can be done here? Well, only one thing: Remove the overloads and check the type at runtime.

```
public static class ExpressionPrinter
{
  public static void Print(Expression e, StringBuilder sb)
  {
    if (e is DoubleExpression de)
    {
      sb.Append(de.Value);
    }
    else if (e is AdditionExpression ae)
    {
      sb.Append("(");
      Print(ae.Left, sb);
      sb.Append("+");
      Print(ae.Right, sb);
      sb.Append(")");
    }
  }
}
```

This is actually a usable solution:

```
var e = new AdditionExpression(
  left: new DoubleExpression(1),
  right: new AdditionExpression(
    left: new DoubleExpression(2),
    right: new DoubleExpression(3)));
var sb = new StringBuilder();
ExpressionPrinter.Print(e, sb);
WriteLine(sb);
```

This approach has a fairly significant downside: There are no compiler checks that you *have*, in fact, implemented printing for every single element in the hierarchy. When a new element gets added, you can keep using `ExpressionPrinter` without modification, and it will just skip over any element of the new type.

This is a viable solution, though. Seriously, it's quite possible to stop here and never go any further in the Visitor pattern: The `is` operator isn't that expensive and I think many developers will remember to cover every single type of object in that `if` statement.

Functional Reflective Visitor

It is worth noting that the approach just adopted is precisely the approach you would adopt in a language such as F#, the only difference being that, of course, instead of inheritance hierarchies you would mainly be dealing with functions.

If, instead of a hierarchy, you defined your expression types in a discriminated union such as

```
type Expression =
  | Add of Expression * Expression
  | Mul of Expression * Expression
  ...
```

then any Visitor you would implement would, most likely, have a structure similar to the following:

```
let rec process expr =
  match expr with
  | And(lhs,rhs) -> ...
  | Mul(lhs,rhs) -> ...
  ...
```

This approach is precisely equivalent to the approach taken in our C# implementation. Each of the cases in a match expression would effectively be turned into an is check. There are major differences, however. First of all, concrete case filters and guard conditions in F# are easier to read than nested if statements in C#. The possible recursiveness of the entire process is a lot more expressive.

Improvements

Although it is not possible to statically enforce the presence of every single necessary type check in the preceding example, it is possible to generate exceptions if the appropriate implementation is missing. To do this, simply make a dictionary that maps the supported types to lambda functions that process those types; that is:

```
private static DictType actions = new DictType
{
  [typeof(DoubleExpression)] = (e, sb) =>
  {
    var de = (DoubleExpression) e;
    sb.Append(de.Value);
  },
  [typeof(AdditionExpression)] = (e, sb) =>
  {
    var ae = (AdditionExpression) e;
    sb.Append("(");
    Print(ae.Left, sb);
    sb.Append("+");
    Print(ae.Right, sb);
    sb.Append(")");
  }
};
```

Now you can implement a top-level `Print()` method in a much simpler fashion. In fact, for bonus points, you can use the C# extension methods mechanic to add `Print()` as a method of any `Expression`:

```
public static void Print(this Expression e, StringBuilder sb)
{
  actions[e.GetType()](e, sb);
}
// sample use:
myExpression.Print(sb)
```

Whether or not you use extension methods or just ordinary static or instance methods on a `Printer` is intirely irrelevant for the purposes of SRP. Both an ordinary class and an extension-method class serve to isolate printing functionality from the data structures themselves, the only difference being whether or not you consider printing part of `Expression`'s API. I personally think this is reasonable: I like the idea of `expression.Print()`, `expression.Eval()`, and so on. If you are an OOP purist, though, you might hate this approach.

What Is Dispatch?

Whenever people speak of visitors, the word *dispatch* is brought up. What is it? Well, put simply, dispatch is a problem of figuring out which methods to call, specifically, how many pieces of information are required to make the call. Here's a simple example:

```
interface IStuff { }
class Foo : IStuff { }
class Bar : IStuff { }

public class Something
{
```

```
  static void func(Foo foo) { }
  static void unc(Bar bar) { }
}
```

Now, if I make an ordinary Foo object, I'll have no problem calling func() with it:

```
Foo foo = new Foo();
func(foo); // this is fine
```

However, if I decide to cast it to a base type (interface or class), the compiler will not know which overload to call:

```
Stuff stuff = new Foo;
func(stuff); // oops!
```

Let's think about this polymorphically: Is there any way we can coerce the system to invoke the correct overload without any runtime (is, as, and similar) checks? It turns out there is.

When you call something on a Stuff, that call can be polymorphic and it can be dispatched right to the necessary component, which in turn can call the necessary overload. This is called *double dispatch* because:

1. First you do a polymorphic call on the actual object.

2. Inside the polymorphic call, you call the overload. Because, inside the object, this has a precise type (e.g., a Foo or Bar), the right overload is triggered.

Here's what I mean:

```
interface Stuff {
  void call();
}
class Foo : Stuff {
  void call() { func(this); }
}
```

```
class Bar : Stuff {
  void call() { func(this); }
}

void func(Foo foo) {}
void func(Bar bar) {}
```

Can you see what is happening here? We cannot just stick one generic call() implementation into Stuff: the distinct implementations must be in their respective classes so that this pointer is suitably typed.

This implementation lets you write the following:

```
Stuff foo = new Foo;
foo.call();
```

Here is a schematic showing what's going on:

```
              this = Foo
foo.call() ------------> func(foo)
```

Dynamic Visitor

Let's return to the ExpressionPrinter example that I claimed has no chance of working:

```
public class ExpressionPrinter
{
  public void Print(AdditionExpression ae, StringBuilder sb)
  {
    sb.Append("(");
    Print(ae.Left, sb);
    sb.Append("+");
    Print(ae.Right, sb);
```

```
  sb.Append(")");
 }

 public void Print(DoubleExpression de, StringBuilder sb)
 {
   sb.Append(de.Value);
 }
}
```

What if I told you I could make it work as is just by adding two keywords and raising the computational cost of the Print(ae,sb) method? I'm sure you can guess what I'm talking about already—dynamic dispatch:

```
public void Print(AdditionExpression ae, StringBuilder sb)
{
  sb.Append("(");
  Print((dynamic)ae.Left, sb);  // <-- look closely here
  sb.Append("+");
  Print((dynamic)ae.Right, sb); // <-- and here
  sb.Append(")");
}
```

The whole business of dynamic was added to C# to support dynamically typed languages. One aspect of some of those languages is the ability to dynamically dispatch; that is, to make call decisions at runtime as opposed to compile time. That's exactly what we're doing here.

Here's how you would call it:

```
var e = ...; // as before
var ep = new ExpressionPrinter();
var sb = new StringBuilder();
ep.Print((dynamic)e, sb); // <-- note the cast here
WriteLine(sb);
```

By casting a variable to dynamic, we defer dispatch decisions until runtime. Thus, we get the correct calls happening; there are only a few problems, namely:

- There is a fairly significant performance penalty related to this type of dispatching.

- If a needed method is missing, you will get a runtime error.

- You can run into serious problems with inheritance.

A dynamic Visitor is a good solution if you expect the object graph you visit to be small and the calls to be infrequent. Otherwise, the performance penalty might make the entire endeavor untenable.

Classic Visitor

The classic implementation of the Visitor design pattern uses *double dispatch*. There are conventions as to what Visitor member functions are called:

- Methods of the Visitor are typically called Visit().

- Methods implemented throughout the hierarchy are typically called Accept().

So now, once again, we have something to put into the base Expression class: the Accept() function.

```
public abstract class Expression
{
  public abstract void Accept(IExpressionVisitor visitor);
}
```

As you can see, this refers to an interface type named IExpressionVisitor that can serve as a base type for various visitors such as ExpressionPrinter, ExpressionEvaluator, and similar. Now, every single implementor of Expression is required to implement Accept() in an identical way, specifically:

```
public override void Accept(IExpressionVisitor visitor)
{
  visitor.Visit(this);
}
```

On the surface of it, this looks like a violation of Don't Repeat Yourself (DRY), another self-descriptive principle. However, if you think about it, every implementor will have a differently typed this reference, so this is not another case of cut-and-paste programming that static analysis tools like to complain about so much.

Now, on the other side, we can define the IExpressionVisitor interface as follows:

```
public interface IExpressionVisitor
{
  void Visit(DoubleExpression de);
  void Visit(AdditionExpression ae);
}
```

Notice that we absolutely must define overloads for all expression objects; otherwise, we would get a compilation error when implementing the corresponding Accept(). We can now implement this interface to define our ExpressionPrinter:

```
public class ExpressionPrinter : IExpressionVisitor
{
  StringBuilder sb = new StringBuilder();
```

```
public void Visit(DoubleExpression de)
{
  sb.Append(de.Value);
}

public void Visit(AdditionExpression ae)
{
  // wait for it!
}

public override string ToString() => sb.ToString();
}
```

The implementation for a DoubleExpression is fairly obvious, but here's the implementation for an AdditionExpression:

```
public void Visit(AdditionExpression ae)
{
  sb.Append("(");
  ae.Left.Accept(this);
  sb.Append("+");
  ae.Right.Accept(this);
  sb.Append(")");
}
```

Notice how the calls now happen on the subexpressions themselves, leveraging double dispatch once again. As for the usage of the new double dispatch Visitor, here it is:

```
var e = new AdditionExpression(
  new DoubleExpression(1),
  new AdditionExpression(
    new DoubleExpression(2),
    new DoubleExpression(3)));
```

```
var ep = new ExpressionPrinter();
ep.Visit(e);
WriteLine(ep.ToString()); // (1 + (2 + 3))
```

Sadly, it's impossible to construct an extension-method analog to this implementation because static classes cannot implement interfaces. If you want to hide the expression printer behind a slightly nicer API, you can go with the following:

```
public static class ExtensionMethods
{
  public void Print(this DoubleExpression e, StringBuilder sb)
  {
    var ep = new ExpressionPrinter();
    ep.Print(e, sb);
  }
  // other overloads here
}
```

Of course, it is up to you to implement all the correct overloads, so this approach doesn't really help much, and provides no safety checks to ensure you've overloaded for every single Expression inheritor.

Implementing an Additional Visitor

What is the advantage of the double dispatch approach? You have to implement the Accept() member through the hierarchy just once. You'll never have to touch a member of the hierarchy again. For example, suppose you now want to have a way of evaluating the result of the expression. This is easy:

```
public class ExpressionCalculator : IExpressionVisitor
{
  public double Result;
```

```
public void Visit(DoubleExpression de)
{
  Result = de.Value;
}

public void Visit(AdditionExpression ae)
{
  // in a moment!
}

// maybe, what you really want is double Visit(...)
}
```

One needs to keep in mind, though, that Visit() is currently declared as a void method, so the implementation for an AdditionExpression might look a little bit weird:

```
public void Visit(AdditionExpression ae)
{
  ae.Left.Accept(this);
  var a = Result;
  ae.Right.Accept(this);
  var b = Result;
  Result = a + b;
}
```

This is a by-product of an inability to return from Accept(), so we cache the results in variables a and b and then return their sum. It works just fine:

```
var calc = new ExpressionCalculator();
calc.Visit(e);
WriteLine($"{ep} = {calc.Result}");
// prints "(1+(2+3)) = 6"
```

The interesting thing about this approach is that you can now write new Visitors, in separate classes, even if you don't have access to the source code of the hierarchy itself. This lets you stay true to both SRP and OCP, in addition to making your code a lot easier to understand.

Acyclic Visitor

Now is a good time to mention that there are actually two strains, if you will, of the Visitor design pattern:

- *Cyclic Visitor,* which is based on function overloading. Due to the cyclic dependency between the hierarchy (which must be aware of the Visitor's type) and the Visitor (which must be aware of every class in the hierarchy), the use of the approach is limited to stable hierarchies that are infrequently updated.

- *Acyclic Visitor,* which is also based on type casting. The advantage here is the absence of limitations on visited hierarchies but, as you might have guessed, there are performance implications.

The first step in the implementation of the Acyclic Visitor is the actual visitor interface. Instead of defining a Visit() overload for every single type in the hierarchy, we make things as generic as possible:

```
public interface IVisitor<TVisitable>
{
  void Visit(TVisitable obj);
}
```

We need each element in our domain model to be able to accept such a Visitor but, because every specialization is unique, what we do is introduce a *marker interface*—an empty interface with absolutely nothing in it.

```
public interface IVisitor {} // marker interface
```

This interface has no members, but we will use it as an argument to an `Accept()` method in whichever object we want to actually visit. Now, what we can do is redefine our `Expression` class from before as follows:

```
public abstract class Expression
{
  public virtual void Accept(IVisitor visitor)
  {
    if (visitor is IVisitor<Expression> typed)
      typed.Visit(this);
  }
}
```

So here's how the new `Accept()` method works: We take an `IVisitor` but then try to cast it to an `IVisitor<T>` where T is the type we're currently in. If the cast succeeds, the visitor in question knows how to visit our type, and so we call its `Visit()` method. If it fails, it's a no-op. It is *critical* to understand why typed itself does not have a `Visit()` that we could call on it. If it did, it would require an overload for every single type that would be interested in calling it, which is precisely what introduces a cyclic dependency.

After implementing `Accept()` in other parts of our model (once again, the implementation in each `Expression` class is identical), we can put everything together by once again defining an `ExpressionPrinter`, but this time around, it would look as follows:

```
public class ExpressionPrinter : IVisitor,
    IVisitor<Expression>,
    IVisitor<DoubleExpression>,
    IVisitor<AdditionExpression>
{
  StringBuilder sb = new StringBuilder();
```

```
public void Visit(DoubleExpression de) { ... }

public void Visit(AdditionExpression ae) { ...  }

public void Visit(Expression obj)
{
  // default handler?
}

public override string ToString() => sb.ToString();
}
```

As you can see, we implement the IVisitor marker interface as well as a Visitor<T> for every T that we like to visit. If we omit a particular type T (e.g., suppose I comment out Visitor<DoubleExpression>), the program will still compile, and the corresponding Accept() call, if it comes, will simply execute as a no-op.

In this case, the implementations of the Visit() methods are identical to what we had in the Classic Visitor implementation, and so are the results.

There is, however, a fundamental difference between this example and the Classic Visitor. The Classic Visitor used an interface, whereas our Acyclic Visitor has an abstract class as the root of the hierarchy. What does this mean? Well, an abstract class can have an implementation that can be used as a fallback, which is why in the definition of ExpressionPrinter, I can implement IVisitor``<Expression> and provide a Visit(Expression obj) method that can be used to handle a missing Visit() overload. For example, you could add logging here, or throw an exception.

Functional Visitor

We already looked at a functional approach to implementing a Visitor when we discussed the Interpreter design pattern, so I do not repeat it here. The general approach boils down to a traversal of a recursive discriminated union using pattern matching on types together with other useful features such as list comprehensions (assuming you're using lists, of course).

The Visitor in a functional paradigm is fundamentally different than the paradigm in OOP. In OOP, a Visitor is a mechanism for giving a set of related classes additional functionality on the side, while ideally being able to do the following:

- Group the functionality together.

- Avoid type checks, instead relying on interfaces.

Pattern matching on a discriminated union is the equivalent of using the is C# keyword (isinst IL instruction) to check each type. Unlike C#, however, F# will tell you about the missing cases, so it offers greater compile-time safety.

Thus, compared to the OOP implementation, the canonical F# visitor would implement a *reflective visitor* approach.

The implementation of Visitor in F# is problematic for many reasons. First, as mentioned before, discriminated unions themselves break the OCP because there is no way to extend them other than to change their definitions. The Visitor implementation compounds the problem further, though: Because our functional Visitor is essentially a huge switch statement, the only way to add support for a particular type is to violate OCP in the Visitor, too.

Summary

The Visitor design pattern allows us to add some distinct behavior to every element in a hierarchy of objects. The approaches we have seen include:

- *Intrusive*: Adding a method to every single object in the hierarchy. This is possible (assuming you have access to source code), but it breaks OCP.

- *Reflective*: Adding a separate Visitor that requires no changes to the objects; this uses is/as whenever runtime dispatch is needed.

- *Dynamic*: Forces runtime dispatch via the DLR by casting hierarchy objects to dynamic. This gives the nicest interface at a very large computational cost.

- *Classic* (double dispatch): The entire hierarchy does get modified, but just once and in a very generic way. Each element of the hierarchy learns to Accept() a Visitor. We then subclass the Visitor to enhance the hierarchy's functionality in all sorts of directions.

- *Acyclic*: Just like the Reflective variety, it performs casting to dispatch correctly. However, it breaks the circular dependency between visitor and visitee and allows for more flexible composition of visitors.

The Visitor appears quite often in tandem with the Interpreter pattern: having interpreted some textual input and transformed it into object-oriented structures, we need to, for example, render the abstract syntax tree in a particular way. Visitor helps propagate a StringBuilder (or similar accumulator object) throughout the entire hierarchy and collate the data together.

Index

A

Abstract Factory
  definition, 69
  IHotDrinkFactory
    interface, 71–72
  interface IHotDrink, 70
  MakeDrink() method, 71
  Prepare() method, 70
Accept() method, 346
ActLike() method, 276
Acyclic visitor
  Expression class, 346
  interface, 345
  IVisitor marker interface, 347
  marker interface, 345
Adapter
  additional storage, 106
  bitmap class, 107
  domain objects, 105
  pattern, 107–109
Add() method, 6, 28, 112, 195
AddChild() method, 45
AddListItem() method, 317
AppendList() method, 316–317
Application programming interface
    (API), 19
Array-backed properties, 238–240

Array of tuples, 116
AsString() method, 152
Autofac dependency injection
    (DI), 100

B

BankAccountCommand
    class, 207, 209–210, 214
Base class, 138–139
Bidirectional Iterator, 237
Bird.Fly() methods, 148
bitmap class, 107
Bridge pattern, 121
Builder pattern
  AddChild() method, 44–45
  communicating internet, 46–47
  constructors, 49
  definition, 41
  DSL construction in F#, 59–60
  fluent interface, 45
  fluent interface inheritance
    class, 55
    implementation, 58
    PersonInfoBuilder, 56, 57
  HtmlElement class, 42–43
  implementation, 42
  in .NET framework, 42

D. Nesteruk, *Design Patterns in .NET*, https://doi.org/10.1007/978-1-4842-4366-4

CPSIA information can be obtained
at www.ICGtesting.com
Printed in the USA
LVHW101948160519
618115LV00004B/6/P